ASPECTS OF THE PASSION

244

By the same author:

Early Christian Creeds   (4th edn Longman, 1982)
Early Christian Doctrines   (5th edn Black, 1977)
Epistles of Peter and of Jude   (Black, 1969)
Jerome: His Life, Writings and Controversies   (Duckworth, 1975)
Pastoral Epistles   (Black, 1963)

ASPECTS OF THE PASSION

by

JOHN N. D. KELLY

FOREWORD BY

LORD RAMSEY
(*a former Archbishop of Canterbury*)

MOWBRAY
LONDON & OXFORD

Copyright © John N. D. Kelly, 1970, 1985

ISBN 0 264 67035 3

First published in 1970 by the
Faith Press as the Archbishop of
Canterbury's Lent Book.

This edition published 1985
by A. R. Mowbray & Co. Ltd,
Saint Thomas House, Becket Street,
Oxford, OX1 1SJ

British Library Cataloguing in Publication Data

Kelly, J.N.D.
  Aspects of the Passion.
  1. Jesus Christ — Passion   2. Bible. N.T.
  Gospels — Commentaries
  I. Title
  232.9'6   BT431

ISBN 0–264–67035–3

Printed in Great Britain by Biddles Ltd. Guildford

CONTENTS

FOREWORD

BY THE MOST REVD ARTHUR MICHAEL RAMSEY

(One hundredth Archbishop of Canterbury, 1961–1974)

AT the heart of the New Testament there stand the story of the Crucifixion and the interpretation of that story by the apostles. For the story, we read the four Gospels; for the interpretation, we read both Gospels and Epistles, to learn how the early Church understood the story in terms of the salvation of the world.

In their understanding of the Cross the apostles used many metaphors and images—sacrifice, covenant, redemption, victory over demons, and others—which are remote from the thought of the modern world. Therein lies the difficulty of the Christian teacher today. Two different solutions of the difficulty are well known. It is possible to cling to the old imagery and present it with insufficient sensitivity to modern minds, or to discard much of the old imagery and retain a few portions of it which modern minds seem likely to assimilate. The former course can give us a Christian teaching orthodox indeed but with little effective contact with modern life. The latter course can give us a watered-down version of Christianity.

In this book Dr. Kelly has chosen a more excellent road, to the benefit of all who will follow it with his guidance. He invites us to a kind of two-way journey. First we go back, with concentrated study, into the language and outlook of the apostles, so as to understand what the Cross meant to them in their thought and experience. Then, we return to the modern world and ask: what does this teaching say to us now in our own lives?

This is therefore a book that demands serious study; it goes deep and is never superficial; it sets us wrestling with the meaning of the Bible. At the same time it is always lucid, and always in touch with the realities of human living. We are helped to see what the Cross means for humanity amidst the frustrations of the twentieth century. I have myself found special value in the third chapter, which tackles one of the most difficulty aspects of the Atonement—the doctrine that the Cross and Resurrection is a divine victory over demonic powers. Dr. Kelly shows how in this case the old imagery comes alive as telling of the answer of the Cross to some of the most frightening aspects of the modern world.

I am sure that those of us who teach and preach about the Cross could not do better than take this book as a guide to the deepening and refreshing of our efforts. It will set us asking whether we are faithful to the many-sided witness of the apostles and whether we are being relevant to our hearers in the present day. I am sure too that all readers who are ready for some discipline in Bible study will find that this book fortifies them in the word of the Cross.

✝ MICHAEL RAMSEY

PREFACE

READING through what I have written, I am deeply conscious of the debt I owe to a host of theologians and New Testament students whose ideas, as a result of constantly reading and lecturing on their works, have infiltrated my own thinking and shaped my attitudes. Echoes of their books will be obvious everywhere to the trained ear, but I feel bound to express my gratitude by name especially to C. K. Barrett, E. Best, J. Burnaby, G. B. Caird, W. D. Davies, C. H. Dodd, J. Knox, R. H. Lightfoot, E. Lohse, J. Macquarrie, J. Moffatt, D. E. Nineham, R. Schnackenburg, and V. Taylor. I could mention others too, not least Michael Ramsey himself, whose *The Glory of God and the Transfiguration of Christ* has always impressed me by its learning and deep spiritual insight. None of these writers, I hasten to add, can be held in any way responsible for the ways in which I have taken up and reacted to their suggestions; but I am sure that every one of them will rejoice, either here or in the world to which they have now passed, if this little book, with all its limitations, should assist people to obtain a clearer understanding of the saving mystery it seeks to expound.

J.N.D.K

St. Edmund's Day, 1969

1

THE CENTRALITY OF THE PASSION

(i)

CHRIST'S passion is, or should be, the focal point of Christian faith and life. In strictness of language the passion denotes his suffering and his death on the cross, but in Christian usage it can legitimately be given a more inclusive significance and be made to embrace the whole drama which revolves around that apparent tragedy. From the commencement of his ministry, the Evangelists suggest, Jesus' eyes were directed towards Calvary; but although Calvary cast its shadow over the preceding weeks and months, it was itself the open door beyond which lay the resurrection. The final act of the drama was not Good Friday but Easter; and Easter stands for the new life through death which both Christ and those who belong to him share, a life which is a reality in the present but which will be consummated in the age to come.

People rightly speak of the cross as embodying the characteristic values of Christianity, reminding us as it does of the Lord's once-for-all sacrifice, and of the resurrection as symbolizing the hope Christianity offers to mankind. But by themselves descriptions like these are one-sided and impoverished because they implicitly regard these events merely as events, deeply significant but somehow external to ourselves. They are part and parcel of our modern habit (modern, but traceable back to an epoch long prior to the Reformation) of isolating Good Friday and Easter from each other, and treating both as commemorative of historical happenings, the one sorrowful and the other resplendent and joyful, which belong to the remote past. The Church of the early centuries was responding to a sounder instinct when it celebrated both as inseparable elements in the one paschal mystery, complementary facets of a redemptive action which is no less effectively operative to-day than in the week when they were first enacted. So St. Augustine, writing in A.D. 400 (Letter 55: 24) could describe Easter as 'the three most sacred days of the Lord's crucifixion, burial, and resurrection.' The truth of the matter is that, understood in its depth and fullness, the passion is an existential experience of the whole body of Christ.

Not surprisingly, therefore, the cross and the resurrection dominate the New Testament and the whole life of the Church, being tacitly presupposed as the determinants of faith even where they are not openly spoken of. In the belief of many scholars the passion narrative embedded in the Gospels was the earliest account of Christ to be put together in a continuous form. In keeping with this the last book of the collection holds up as its hero the Risen Lord who 'makes all things new' (Rev. 21: 5), who is also 'the Lamb that has been slain' and who, though he has triumphed, still displays the marks of his martyrdom (Rev. 5: 5–12). St. Paul's chief ambition is (Phil. 3: 10) 'that I may know Christ and the power of his resurrection, and may share his sufferings, becoming like him in his death.' So when a man or a woman becomes a Christian, he or she is signed with Christ's cross in baptism and thus enters on his resurrection life. And when Christians meet together, week by week or even day by day, they manifest their fellowship with one another and with God by sharing the broken bread and outpoured wine in which Christ's passion is shown forth and the Lord makes himself known to each one of them.

(ii)

What are Christians to-day to make of Christ's passion and resurrection? In every age, in so far as men and women have identified themselves with them, they have found themselves achieving that mastery over fate and life's cruellest blows, that emancipation from self and its enslavements, which St. John

calls (1 John 5: 4) 'overcoming the world'; and each generation, from its own concrete situation, has made its own contribution to our understanding of the strange sequence of
events. In attempting ourselves to absorb their impact we have
a variety of approaches open to us, each making an appeal to
a different kind of temperament. Some, for example, might
prefer an objectively historical discussion; they would like to
see the several narratives compared, their apparent divergences
sorted out and explained, and the record of what actually
happened established in its contemporary setting. Others with
a more speculative cast of mind might welcome a survey of
the theology, or rather the theologies, of the passion which
Christian thinkers, in earlier ages or in more recent times,
have constructed with the object of elucidating the mystery
and its many-sided significance.

Either of these approaches, as well as others that might be
suggested, would be interesting and instructive, but in this
book we have chosen to follow a different path. For their
knowledge of what occurred in the first Holy Week and Easter
Christians are entirely dependent on the New Testament
accounts; and whatever theological conclusions they work out
about the meaning of Christ's death and resurrection, these
must all in the end be tested by the New Testament witness.
Our proposal therefore is to return to the New Testament
itself, opening ourselves to its influence and seeking to enter
into the minds and thoughts of the men who wrote it. Since
everything that happens in history happens once for all and
cannot be repeated, the passion itself necessarily eludes our
scrutiny; but the New Testament contains not only the most
primitive records of what took place, but also the interpretations put upon it by people who had been in close contact
with the original eye-witnesses. And it may be a reinvigora-
ting exercise to turn aside for a while from current confused
and often negative debates about Christianity, and refresh
ourselves from the sources.

Thus in the following chapters we shall be singling out and

reflecting on, one after another, the most characteristic and important of these interpretations in the attempt to discover how they can illuminate the saving events for us. A good deal of patience, concentration and imaginative responsiveness will be required, for the Bible yields useful insights only to minds which are prepared to be receptive. We should not be surprised or deterred if some of these ways of looking at the passion strike us, on first examination at any rate, as paradoxical, puzzling or uncongenial to our usual modes of thought. It is only to be expected that the New Testament writers, living in a totally different intellectual climate from ours, should have presuppositions and employ imagery which we find unfamiliar and hard to assimilate. The task incumbent upon us (and we can be sure that it is a rewarding one) is to make the effort to pierce through this veil of unaccustomed imagery and seize the realities which lie behind it.

(iii)

In making this effort present-day Christians are in at least two respects more advantageously placed than their predecessors of last century, or even of the first half of this. First, recent decades have seen the gradual re-emergence, in reaction to the extravagant individualism which held the stage from the Renaissance onwards, of a consciousness of the intrinsic unity, or solidarity, of human beings with one another. Inherited assumptions die hard, but it is at least no longer regarded as axiomatic that each man or woman is an isolated, autonomous entity, cut off from and without responsibilities towards other members of the race except in so far as society or his own decision creates obligations, and free in principle to develop his personality exactly as he pleases.

All sorts of factors, ranging from our more sensitive appreciation of racial memory and community psychology to the shortening of communications, have contributed to the weakening of this notion. But perhaps the most obvious practical token of the change is the almost personal involvement which people nowadays increasingly feel in events (wars, natural disasters, starvation and poverty, political injustice) which happen, it may be, at the other end of the world from themselves and for which no direct responsibility could possibly be attributed to them. For the writers of the New Testament, as for most of those of the Old, the solidarity of mankind was a truth which was taken for granted. They accepted without question that what was done by one individual, or what happened to him, could have repercussions, for good or for evil, far beyond himself and his immediate circle.

Secondly, although there is much talk among professional theologians and humanist intellectuals about man's having 'come of age' and being master of his fate, there is little or no echo of this among the masses of ordinary people. On the contrary, there is a widespread sense of bafflement and frustration, of alienation and of being at the mercy of uncontrollable forces, which makes the present age an anxious and even despairful one. The old certainties have melted away, and so far from having the adult self-confidence their fathers enjoyed, many people feel like children in the dark who cannot find their way home. As a by-product of this, social unrest and even violence have been unleashed in many countries, some of them commonly esteemed the most civilized, on a scale unprecedented for generations, and have inevitably heightened the prevalent sense of insecurity. Symptomatic also of our deep-seated confusion and lack of certainty about ultimate things are the curious contradictions which make current attitudes so ambivalent. Thus we have the self-same people claiming that absolute morality has been explained away, and in the next breath vigorously denouncing cruelty, injustice and exploitation; and in the same newspaper we can read the report of a rationalist congress in one column, and in the next the advice which an expert in astrology purveys week by week to his circle of anxiously waiting devotees.

Many of these features, so painfully familiar to us but so

shocking to the optimistic presuppositions of the liberal era, find striking analogies in the world in which the New Testament writers lived and suffered and found their way to Christ. As a result, in spite of the vast differences (economic, political, technological, and the like) between their environment and ours, it is scarcely surprising that the terms in which the human predicament presented itself to them were in many respects similar. Even if there were no other reason, therefore, it would for this reason alone be profitable for us to study the passion through their eyes.

(iv)

There is, however, another reason, and one of immense importance: these first-century Christians were sustained by an intense conviction which modern Christians, even those who count themselves most traditional and orthodox, have largely lost. This was the conviction, of which echoes can be heard throughout the New Testament, that with the death and resurrection of Christ a new and glorious era had been ushered in. For them these were not events—awesome, amazing, profoundly significant, but still events—which took their place in the endless sequence of historical occurrences; as apprehended by the eye of faith, they had brought history, in the ordinary sense of the word, to an end. Thus they had the exultant consciousness of living in the long expected age of God's final revelation, an age which would reach its triumphant climax with Christ's coming again on the Last Day but in whose blessings the believing Church participates now. We have an illustration of this in St. Paul's description (1 Cor. 10: 11) of his generation as one upon whom 'the end of the ages has come,' another in his exclamation (2 Cor. 6: 2), 'See, now is the acceptable time, now is the day of salvation,' and yet a third in St. Peter's teaching (1 Pet. 4: 7 and 5: 1) that 'the end of all things has arrived,' and that he himself is already 'a partaker in the glory that is going to be revealed.'

Admittedly affirmations like these introduce us to a complex of ideas (about this age and the age to come, the Messianic kingdom, and the like) which were accepted naturally enough in the predominantly Jewish milieu in which Christianity was cradled, but which demand scholarly elucidation before modern people can fully appreciate them; in the New Testament itself we can observe them being silently reformulated in different idioms as later writers, with a more Gentile cultural background, take them over. Nevertheless there shines through them, unmistakable behind the historically conditioned wrappings, the confident assurance that Christ is the turning-point in history; his death and resurrection mark the transition from one world-order to another, and open up wonderful, undreamed of possibilities for the individual as for mankind. This is a confidence we can at least begin to recover if we allow our minds to be moulded by the thought of the New Testament writers on the passion.

2

DIVINE NECESSITY

(i)

WHEN modern people read or listen to the story of Christ's passion, they are frequently shocked by its apparent senselessness, and filled with revulsion at the hatred and cynicism which conspired to bring about the execution of so holy and heroic a figure. His sufferings excite their pity, and since the middle ages both popular books of devotion and religious art have dwelt on them in realistic, sometimes morbid detail. In keeping with this the hymns we sing, the addresses we hear, and the liturgy the clergy perform in Lent and Passiontide tend to be steeped in gloom, and the atmosphere of our churches becomes increasingly charged with mournful foreboding.

These are understandable reactions, but they are far from being the ones most characteristic of the New Testament. Indeed there is no evidence at all that the apostolic writers regarded the passion as just one more of those acts of meaningless brutality which besmirch human history. They certainly did not conceal their indignation against those who condemned Jesus. Thus a very early text of St. Paul's such as 1 Thess. 2: 14–15 ('. . . the Jews, who killed both the Lord Jesus and the prophets . . . and displease God') illustrates their disgust that the Messiah had been done to death by his own people, and this motif becomes progressively more prominent, especially in the Fourth Gospel. As the first century advances we can also trace, for example in the way the Evangelists highlight the crown of thorns, the scourging and the insults heaped on Jesus, a sharpening interest in his physical humiliation and agony. But these concerns always remain relatively subordinate and peripheral in the New

18

Testament, and throw little or no light on its authors' deeper understanding of the passion.

An illuminating clue to this is provided by a fragment of primitive preaching which St. Paul has preserved for us in 1 Cor. 15: 3-4. We know that it has this character, for the Apostle reminds his readers that it represents the gospel which he had himself been taught and had in his turn handed on to them. It is to the effect that 'Christ died for our sins in accordance with the scriptures, that he was buried, that he was raised on the third day in accordance with the scriptures.' The whole statement is immensely significant, but it is only the repeated phrase 'in accordance with the scriptures' which claims our attention in this section. It reveals that, so far from regarding the death of Jesus as a pointless tragedy, or as simply the product of human hostility and violence, the apostolic Church believed it to have been foreshadowed in the Old Testament, indeed to have been the divinely contrived prelude to his exaltation. Wicked men, with their petty jealousies and squalid ambitions, were certainly its immediate instruments, but behind the entire transaction lay the holy will of God accomplishing its mysterious purpose.

Startling though it may at first appear to us, we have to recognize that this idea, expounded in a variety of forms, is a New Testament commonplace. It appears, for example, in Acts 2: 23, which may well embody another excerpt of very primitive preaching and which speaks of Jesus as having been 'delivered up according to the definite plan and foreknowledge of God,' and again in St. Peter's comparison (1 Pet. 1: 19-20) of Christ to a sacrificial lamb which has been marked out for this role before the foundation of the world. It is, however, even more graphically presented in St. Luke's Gospel, in the strange story (Luke 24: 13-27) of the two disciples who, without at first recognizing him, encountered the Risen Lord as they walked to Emmaus. When they had gloomily described their distress at the ignominious end of the man they had hoped would redeem Israel, and how confused they were by the rumours circulating that he was in fact still alive, the stranger rebuked them for their lack of perception, and explained that what had occurred was exactly what the prophets had foretold. If only they had understood the scriptures correctly, they would have realized that it was 'necessary that the Christ should suffer these things and enter into his glory.'

(ii)

This is an aspect which is worth our pondering, and for a fuller and more systematic treatment of it we should turn to St. Mark. Although his Gospel at first sight looks like a straightforward account of Jesus' ministry, and although it is undoubtedly built up out of reminiscences of his actions and sayings, it is seen on closer inspection to be a careful and relatively sophisticated attempt to explain the paradox of the cross to people who believed Jesus to be the Messiah. A nineteenth-century scholar once called it 'a passion narrative with an extended introduction'; and the accuracy of this description is borne out by the fact that, although the passion and resurrection are confined to only three chapters (14–16), the preceding thirteen are filled with premonitions of them. St. Mark is as conscious as any one of the suffering and disgrace Jesus had to endure; it is precisely these that confront him with his problem. Nor does he try to minimize the part played in bringing them about by human malevolence; as early as his third chapter (3: 6), he underlines the determination of the Pharisees and Herodians to destroy Jesus. At the same time no New Testament writer has such an unshakeable conviction that from start to finish the passion represented the unfolding of a divine plan; it was a journey through the night of pain and ignominy which God himself had prescribed, and which therefore was bound to issue in a glorious sequel.

Perhaps the most eloquent proof of this conviction is the way St. Mark repeatedly reminds us that Jesus was himself fully aware of the cross as a divine necessity and accepted it as such. Quite early in the ministry, when people are wondering why Jesus' disciples take no part in the conventional fasts, he represents (2: 19–20) the Master, still unrecognized in his true role, as explaining that the appropriate time for them to fast will be 'when the Bridegroom is taken away from them.' The Jewish authorities have not yet begun to plot Jesus' removal, but he is already apprised of the doom overhanging him. But it is after St. Peter's acknowledgment of his Messiahship that the Lord is portrayed (8: 29) as speaking to his companions with complete frankness about his approaching passion. 'He began to teach them,' we read (8: 31–2), 'that the Son of man must suffer many things . . . and be killed, and after three days rise again. And he stated this plainly.' In the next chapter we find him twice over repeating the identical prediction, once after his Transfiguration (9: 12) and once as he is travelling through Galilee (9: 31). Not surprisingly, the disciples are dumbfounded with incredulity; but a little later, as the party sets out on the fateful journey to Jerusalem with Jesus striding ahead, he warns his stupefied associates a fourth time (10: 33–4) that the Son of man is going to be insulted, brutally maltreated and condemned to death, and that he will rise again.

A feature which has always struck readers of these accounts is the Evangelist's choice of the strong verb 'must' and other phrases of similar import. Long before his passion, it is suggested, Jesus was aware that death inevitably awaited him, but he discerned God's controlling hand in the fateful chain of events. Once the actual drama commences, this impression of divine necessity is greatly enhanced. Again and again the Old Testament prophecies are appealed to. Thus at the Last Supper Jesus announces (14: 21) that 'the Son of man goes as it is written of him'; and when after supper the disciples and he are walking on the Mount of Olives, he recalls (14: 27) Zechariah's prophecy that the shepherd would be struck down and the sheep scattered. As he expires on the cross, he quotes (15: 34) a verse from Psalm 22 ('My God, my God, why have you forsaken me?') which implies that he finds his own abandonment, and also his ultimate deliverance, prefigured in the experience of the Psalmist. At the same time the Evangelist represents Jesus as having an accurate foreknowledge of everything that is going to befall him. He knows (14: 18, 27–31) that one of his chosen circle will betray him, and that the whole group, the protesting Peter not excepted, will fall away. In the devotion of the woman who poured her jar of ointment over his head he detects (14: 3–9) a symbolic anticipation, almost a rehearsal, of the anointing of his body for burial. He is confident (14: 28) that after his death he will be raised up, and will appear again to his followers in Galilee.

(iii)

Viewed in this light, St. Mark's portrayal of the passion as a divine necessity which has been forecast in precise detail in scripture is an extraordinary one. Why should he, and the other New Testament writers who shared the same attitude, single out the death of Jesus as manifesting in a special way the accomplishment of God's designs? In any case, what beneficial objectives could they imagine the divine purpose to be achieving by it? In every corner of the world brutality and murder are everyday occurrences; men and women are always being humiliated, done to death, driven to despair or overwhelmed by cruel disasters brought about either by the callousness and malignity of their fellows, or by the impersonal pressures of circumstance. That is the way this unhappy world works; and so far from detecting the gracious activity of God in the crazy tragedy, most reflective people regard it as one of the principal obstacles to faith. In later chapters we shall be trying to analyse more closely the New Testament writers' interpretation of Christ's passion as the realization of God's beneficent purposes. The question which first demands an answer is what they meant when they claimed that he, uniquely among mankind, had suffered 'according to the scriptures.'

First, we must understand that in the view of each one of them Jesus was no ordinary person. For them all he was the Messiah or anointed representative of God, the Lord whose supernatural status and mandate they sought to convey to their readers by means of a whole series of exalted images. To St. Mark, for example, whose approach we have been chiefly considering, the title which seems most appropriate for him is Son of God. His book begins (1: 1) with the announcement that it is 'the gospel of Jesus Christ, the Son of God,' and it reaches its climax with the centurion's confession (15: 39), 'This man was in truth the Son of God.' At the key-moments of his baptism (1: 11) and his Transfiguration (9: 7) the heavenly voice proclaims, first to Jesus himself and then in the hearing of the three disciples who were his closest associates, that he is God's 'unique Son.'

Nor was this conviction of St. Mark's, any more than the adoring devotion of other first-century Christians, the product of excited imagination or disordered fantasy. As all the Gospels make evident, it sprang from and rested upon the impact which Jesus had made on the people around him, among whom he lived and worked. By his words and actions, by the things he said about himself, above all by the compulsive authority of his person, they had been brought to realize that he was (as St. Peter was led to declare at Caesarea Philippi: Matt. 16: 16) 'the Christ, the Son of the living God.' True, this faith of theirs had been temporarily shattered by the shock of his execution; but it had been restored, firm and unshakeable, by the overwhelming evidence they had afterwards received that he had been raised from the dead and was alive for evermore.

Secondly, we must remember that the Church of the first century had Israel as its womb; as Israel's child it inherited not only its hopes and aspirations, but also its understanding of God. Christianity can never afford to forget that it is the mature flowering of the revelation earlier given to God's chosen people, the Jews, or fail to take that revelation seriously. Guided by God's disclosure of himself as set out in the Old Testament, the Evangelists and the other New Testament writers instinctively grasped that his age-old purpose was the emergence of a holy people consecrated to his service, and that in a world dominated as it is by sin his people would only be able to fulfil its appointed role by undergoing humiliation and suffering. Indeed its trials and tribulations were, in some mysterious way, the divinely ordered means by which evil would eventually be overcome and 'new heavens and a new earth in which righteousness dwells' (2 Pet. 3: 13) established. And in a special degree these trials would be the lot of the Messiah, the leader and representative of God's people, who would supremely express in his person at once their high vocation, their poignant experience, and their glorious destiny.

It was Jesus himself, according to the Evangelists, who first emphasized that this was the profound truth to which the Old Testament, with its record of God's dealings with men, was consistently pointing. At first, expecting (like many of their contemporaries) the Messiah to be a victorious figure who would set up a dazzling earthly kingdom, the disciples found it repellant and unpalatable; but as their conviction deepened that Jesus was indeed the Chosen One and spoke with divine authority, their initial revulsion was overcome. They came to perceive that the essential message, not of certain isolated texts but of scripture as a whole, was crystallized in the suffering and resurrection of their Lord.

(iv)

It is imperative that, in seeking to penetrate the significance of the passion, modern Christians should enter as fully and sympathetically as possible into the mentality of the apostolic writers and view it from their standpoint. Unless they can apprehend it as fulfilling, however mysteriously,

God's eternal counsel, they are likely to dismiss it as a tragic enigma or even a pathetic futility. The Christians of the first century certainly had one enormous advantage over us in reaching their inspired insight. Brought up in the religion of Israel, it was in no way astonishing to them that God should employ historical persons and events to accomplish his designs. Having known Jesus or others who had had direct contact with him, and having reacted to the power which radiated from his personality, they did not find it paradoxical to affirm (Heb. 1: 1–2) that God, who 'spoke in former times to our fathers by the prophets . . . , has in these last days spoken to us by a Son.' Accustomed, too, to the idea of divine intervention, they were not only able, in the light of the compelling evidence adduced, to accept the Lord's resurrection as a fact, but felt justified in interpreting it as clinching proof of God's deliberate vindication of his own.

The secularized men and women of to-day have been differently conditioned; they are taken aback by the suggestion that history should have any pattern at all, much less a pattern traced by God's hand and exhibiting the working out, stage by stage, of a carefully prearranged divine programme. Yet for Christianity, just as much as for the Judaism of the Old Testament, it is a cardinal premiss that all history is salvation history. Thus the cross and the empty tomb can be hailed as the focal points where God's saving purpose is most unambiguously and eloquently, though to unenlightened eyes obscurely, set forth. We are faced here, of course, with a clash of fundamental attitudes, but if we are Christians we are bound to ask ourselves, when we are tempted to exclude divine purpose from human life and history, whether we are not making unwarranted concessions to the spirit of the age and acquiescing uncritically in a prejudice which squares ill with our other convictions.

Certainly, if the God we believe in is personal and active, if he is the God of whom we have learned from Jesus Christ, it seems unreasonable that we should so drastically limit the scope of his operation. And if, through contemplating the person of Jesus and meditating on his passion as delineated in the New Testament, we can discern, however glimmeringly, the action of God at work in his death and resurrection, we shall not only begin to make sense of those entirely unique and special events, but shall be on the way to discovering the clue to the more commonplace problems of our own lives too. For it is integral to the gospel message that the holy purpose of God is being worked out not only in the passion of his Son, but in the whole experience, whether of sorrow or joy, of disappointment or achievement, of the people who belong to him and seek to conform themselves to his will.

3

VICTORY OVER EVIL

(i)

WHILE the New Testament writers generally were certain that the passion of Christ had been brought about 'according to the definite plan and foreknowledge of God' (Acts 2: 23), they were as much concerned as we to formulate in more precise terms both the nature of this plan and the effects it achieved. As we study their writings, we can observe various theories being sketched out, and sometimes it is obvious that two or three alternative explanations are criss-crossing in the mind of the same writer. We shall now attempt to disentangle the more interesting of these, examining them separately and seeking to translate them into thought-forms more congenial to our age. We shall begin with an approach which has left a deep imprint on the New Testament itself, but which has often been passed over in classic expositions of the work of Christ. One reason for this neglect is that, while accepted without question in the first century, the system of ideas with which it seemed to be logically tied up came to be rejected by later generations. The theory we have in mind is the doctrine that Christ's passion and resurrection represent the decisive victory of God over the cosmic forces of evil.

Even a casual reader of the Gospels cannot help noticing how prominent in the Evangelists' minds is the idea that one of the principal tasks of the Messiah is to do battle with Satan and the wicked demons who served as his agents. As they see it, this is the significance of Jesus' temptations; at the very commencement of his ministry he is confronted by the Adversary face to face in the wilderness, and wins an initial victory. This is also in their eyes the key to his cures of unhappy people possessed by devils, for these tormentors of theirs are the minions of Satan. As the ministry proceeds, these preliminary but signally successful skirmishes with Satan are taken as reliable proof that the kingdom of God for which good men yearned is at last being inaugurated. As Jesus himself points out (Matt. 12: 28), 'If I am casting out demons by the Spirit of God, then has God's kingdom come upon you.'

It is in his passion and death, however, that the grim struggle reaches its climax. In describing these events, St. Luke explicitly states (22: 3–6) that it was Satan who instigated Judas to turn traitor and arrange for the betrayal; and when the arrest is made he represents (22: 53) Jesus as admitting that for the moment 'the power of darkness' has prevailed. St. John too, in his Gospel, speaks (13: 27) of Satan using Judas as his pawn, but sets the picture in a larger and richer perspective by reporting (12: 31) Jesus' statement that 'Now is the judgment of this world, now shall the ruler of this world be cast out.' Like the other Evangelists, he discerns in Christ's ministry, and supremely in his passion and resurrection, the decisive action of God subduing and bringing into order a demonic and rebellious creation.

(ii)

Long before the Gospels were written down, a closely related picture, with colourful elaboration and a more cosmic slant, was being painted in the theology of St. Paul. As he envisages it, the created universe has passed into enemy control, the occupying forces being Satan and the wicked spirits associated with him. The modern reader is given an uncomfortable jolt by his description of the former as 'the god of this world' who 'has blinded unbelievers' minds' (2 Cor. 4: 4), or as 'the prince of the power of the air, the spirit who is now at work in the sons of disobedience' (Eph. 2: 2). Even more startling are his references to 'the rulers of this age' (1 Cor. 2: 6 and 8), or 'the elemental spirits' to whom his readers were enslaved before their conversion (Gal. 4: 9), or 'the spiritual hosts of wickedness in the heavenly places' (Eph. 6: 12). Evidently the Apostle conceives of the existing world-order as lying under the sway of these supernatural beings and their leader. It is they who are the real frustraters of God's will, the true enemies against whom the Christian has to contend; and so he urges his correspondents (Eph. 6: 13–17) to equip themselves with the whole panoply of spiritual armour, all the weapons of faith and saving virtue that God supplies.

St. Paul can press his exhortation with confidence, for he is convinced that, provided they have followed his advice, they have nothing to fear. The reason is that, by his dying and rising again, Christ has already shattered the might of the hostile array, and the Christian who has enrolled under his banner can share the fruits of his triumph. Several passages enable us to glimpse how he conceived this victory to have been obtained. In one (1 Cor. 2: 7–8), for example, we read that God had a secret plan for our glorification, decreed before the ages, but the supernatural powers who tried to thwart it failed to recognize who Jesus really was and crucified him; the implication is that his resurrection spelled their overthrow. In another (Col. 2: 15) the Apostle depicts the Risen Lord as disarming his persecutors, making a public mockery of them, and leading them in his triumphal procession. But his fullest and most eloquent account is the one contained in the hymn-like strophes of the second chapter of Philippians (2: 6–11). These declaim how Christ, though it was open to him to retain his divine status, deliberately humbled himself to the level of our humanity and with unswerving obedience submitted to a shameful death on the cross. The outcome was that God raised him to the heights, assigning him the supreme title of Lord and causing every being in heaven, on earth and under the earth (our demonic adversaries, it is implied, included) to yield him allegiance.

This conception of the passion and resurrection as a conflict with evil forces resulting in their disastrous overthrow is far from being confined to the Evangelists and St. Paul. We catch a strong echo of it in the Epistle to the Hebrews, which explains (2: 14–15) that the purpose of the incarnation was that, through himself undergoing death, Christ 'might reduce to impotence him who has power to inflict death, that is, the devil, and liberate those who, through dread of death, were subject to lifelong slavery.' How this is achieved the writer does not elucidate, but he probably envisages the devil as overreaching his authority by inflicting death on the Son of God.

The same exultant note of triumph resounds through the First Epistle of Peter. The object of this short, vigorous letter is to stiffen the morale of scattered Christian communities in Asia Minor which are passing through a terrifying period of harassment, victimization and positive persecution at the hands of their pagan neighbours. Throughout the writer's theme is that his readers can afford to be quietly confident, for Christ has already vanquished the malefic spirits whose instruments their human persecutors are. His exhortation reaches its climax in an obscure and often misunderstood passage in chapter 3 (verses 18–22). The meaning of this, correctly interpreted, is that Christ also has had to suffer, like the Christians in Asia Minor, and indeed as incarnate man has been put to death; but having been raised from the dead, he has ascended to God's right hand and has proclaimed to the evil spirits, as he passed through the lower heavens where they are imprisoned, that their harsh sway over mankind has been broken once for all and that spiritual beings of every rank are now subject to him alone. Through their baptism the Asian Christians are associated with him in his triumph.

(iii)

To many modern Christians this particular approach to the passion is apt to seem puzzling, not to say disconcerting. As set out in the New Testament it is admittedly part and parcel of a world view, of a theory about the existence and function of supernatural agencies, and of assumptions about the origin of evil which have all become superseded and almost meaningless. The New Testament writers, it is plain, had taken over from their cultural background a conception of the structure of the universe and its occupants which is totally foreign to us. Like many of their contemporaries, they believed the earth, the abode of men, to be a body moving freely in space with a plurality of heavens ranged in order above it. Moreover, they accepted the view that the act of creation had involved God in a tremendous struggle against chaos and the forces of evil, and that although he had emerged victorious the malefic powers had to some extent reasserted their sway over his creation. With their leader, Satan, they dominated the heavenly spheres immediately above the earth, having their dwelling on the planets, and from this vantage-point held mankind in their tyrannical grip, manipulating its destiny and instigating individuals to acts of wickedness and blasphemy. Only the intervention of God himself, through his appointed emissary, could loosen their hold and subjugate them; and this decisive victory, the first-century Christians believed, he had accomplished through the incarnation, passion and resurrection of Christ.

This, or something like this, is the framework of ideas which the writers at whose theology of the passion we have been glancing took for granted, and within which they elaborated their picture of Christ as conqueror of the perverted fiends who have enslaved man. What are we to make of it? In the judgment of many we should dismiss it as obsolete mythology, since feature after feature in it is alien from our thinking and corresponds to nothing that we know of reality. But we should hesitate to take this drastic step. Myth the framework undoubtedly is, but myth is often the vehicle by means of which men apprehend profound truths which are not easily formulated in direct speech. The imagery it employs may come to seem outmoded and even bizarre, but it may contain a message which, transposed into different and more sympathetic images, can be seen to have permanent significance and validity. This is certainly true of the New Testament portrait of Christ as the vanquisher of the devil and his wicked angels. Reinterpreted in the changing thought-forms of succeeding centuries, it dominated Christian reflection on the work of Christ for a thousand years. With its symbolism appropriately modified, it contains a wealth of meaning for Christians in the twentieth century too.

(iv)

To give but two examples, the ideas of a primeval rebellion of created spirits against God have completely faded for modern men and women, along with the primitive cosmology which the New Testament writers accepted without question. So too have those other stories or myths of the fall of man, the origin of evil, and the corruption of the natural order which left a deep imprint on earlier Christian thinking. Nevertheless when we contemplate the prodigality of nature, its openness to exploitation, and its cold obliviousness to values of whatever kind, we can sense the force of St. Paul's statement (Rom. 8: 19–22) that the whole sub-human creation has been made subject to futility, and is only waiting 'to be rescued from its bondage to decay.' As regards man himself, the sense of alienation and lostness, of being at odds with his own nature and his neighbours, and separated from the true source of his being which, if we are Christians, we know to be God, is just as real and poignant an existential experience to-day as it was in the first century. Though modern man uses different language to describe it, or else feels dumb and inarticulate, he is no less conscious of living in a disordered world which fails to satisfy, but which none the less dangles before him a host of desirable objects which fatally wrest from him his allegiance. It does not come naturally to us to personify these, but we find ourselves in effect treating as gods or demons things which are emphatically not God.

Again, if we are asked to take their words literally, the New Testament writers seem to us to be spinning fairy-tales when they talk of 'principalities and powers' installed on the planets and manipulating human beings like puppets. So at least we commonly think; but the time may be nearer than we dare guess when a situation all too closely resembling this may be frighteningly realized. This is an era of space rivalry, and millions are thrilled by the achievements of adventurous astronauts who sweep at incredible speeds through the heavens to encircle and ultimately land on the moon. But one of the ambitious projects coolly contemplated by the governments which finance and direct these operations is the stationing of platforms in space from which they may survey the earth's surface and, in the end, exert despotic control over the lives and policies of their fellow-men.

But even if we leave such terrifying possibilities out of account, there have been few ages when ordinary people have had a more helpless sense of being at the mercy of invisible, intangible, utterly unpredictable and seemingly unconcerned determinants of their fate than the present. Sometimes it is something natural and inevitable that appals us, like death, disease or accident. Sometimes it is the social or international conflicts which have been so frequent and disastrous in recent times, and against which the individual can do virtually nothing. Society itself, whether considered as a pervasive influence reducing every one to unquestioning conformity, or more narrowly as the highly organized state which under modern conditions, with its network of bureaucratic subdivisions, concentrates irresistible power in the government of the day, increasingly imposes shackles on private persons, and only with extreme reluctance concedes any appeal to a higher law.

The sense of insecurity is magnified by the realization that man's escalating achievements in physical science and technology are making him the defenceless victim of his own discoveries. Historians have described the first century and its immediate successors as an age of anxiety, but the description is coming to apply at least as aptly to our own. Again we do not naturally picture the causes of our anxiety, the forces which seem to dominate our lives so capriciously, as relentless angels or demons; but the realities for which those images stand are no less authentic and painful in our experience.

Stripped of metaphor and symbolism, the essence of the New Testament affirmation that Christ is the heroic conqueror of the demons that plague mankind is that, as God's representative who has suffered and died and been raised from the dead, he has transformed the tragic aspect of the human condition. By himself overcoming the frustrations which hold us immobile in their grip (whether pictured naïvely as wicked spirits, or envisaged more realistically as impersonal forces or destructive propensities in our own make-up), he has opened up the possibility of our doing likewise. The texts we have so far discussed have not explained, except in mythological terms, how he has done this, but the New Testament writers are not without illuminating suggestions of a different kind, and we shall be examining some of these in subsequent chapters. In the meantime we should note that the whole magnificent conception of Christ as the vanquisher of evil and the liberator of mankind from bondage is not one which can in the last resort be validated by rationalistic analysis; it rests on two convictions which spring from and are nourished by Christian faith. The first is the perception that in Christ there is a movement of God towards the created order, a genuine and voluntary entering of the divine into human life and identification of itself with the human condition so that thereby it can be radically altered. The second is the belief that, as the consequence of Christ's gracious acceptance of this role and in effect making himself in all respects one of us, we human beings can by faith enter into fellowship with the divine and so transcend the limitations of our lot.

4

REDEMPTIVE SACRIFICE

(i)

IF it stood by itself, the affirmation that Christ, Son of God as
he is, has vanquished the evil forces that dominate man and
have fastened their grip on the created order clearly requires
further elucidation, not least because of the paradox that
suffering and death are regarded as essential ingredients in
the transaction. First-century Christians were fully alive to
this, and the New Testament shows how, by drawing out and
focusing attention on certain features of the passion, they felt
able to envisage it as contributing to Christ's victory.

Perhaps the most prominent and characteristic of these
approaches was their portrayal of it as a sacrificial action, an
acceptable offering which obtained forgiveness for the human
race and made reconciliation between God and his alienated
creation possible. As we noticed in Chapter II (i), this idea is
present in the fragment of extremely primitive preaching
preserved in 1 Cor. 15: 3, which asserts that 'Christ died for
our sins.' There are few books of the New Testament from
which sacrificial language is lacking, and it is noteworthy that
in the last one the imagery of sacrifice alternates with that of
triumph. For the author of Revelation Christ is the victor who
reassures his faithful servants with the promise (3: 21), 'Him
who conquers I will permit to sit with me on my throne, as I
myself have conquered and have sat down with my Father on
his throne'; but he is also 'the Lamb who was slain' (5: 12),
the slaughtered victim in whose blood the martyrs 'have
washed their robes and made them clean' (7: 14).

For modern people 'sacrifice,' except in the context of
traditional Christian piety, either conjures up the crude and
distasteful rites of immature religions or has become an over-

worked, devalued metaphor. For first-century Christians, however, it was natural, and indeed unavoidable, that they should resort to the term, with the ideas and imagery which clustered around it, in seeking to provide a rationale of Christ's passion. In the contemporary world the category of sacrifice, though criticized in sophisticated circles, was by and large taken for granted; it was by making appropriate offerings to God that men maintained or renewed their right relationship with him. The New Testament writers had been brought up in a Jewish ambience, and the Old Testament books were their venerated scriptures. They knew that when he had made the covenant with his chosen people at Mount Sinai, it had been sealed with sacrifices and the shedding of blood (see Exodus 24: 3–8). Year by year the marvellous deliverance of Israel from Egypt was celebrated by the Passover sacrifice, and it is obvious that the folk memory of the Exodus was deeply imprinted on their consciousness. The Law, they knew, had not only prescribed a multitude of sacrifices by individuals on specific occasions, but also made provision for daily offerings in the Temple on behalf of the whole community; and there was the special ritual on the annual Day of Atonement, when sacrifices were offered for the sin of the people during the year. Very soon Christians came to realize that, since the coming of Christ, they were no longer bound by these holy observances. It is understandable, however, that their religious thinking should be conditioned by the concept or model of sacrifice; and since it was precisely the passion and death of Jesus that had rendered the older system of worship obsolete for them, it was inevitable that they should transfer the imagery of sacrifice to them.

(ii)

The idea of the passion as a redemptive sacrifice appears in various forms in the New Testament, and according to St. Mark's account is traceable to our Lord himself. We recall his great saying (Mark 10: 45), pronounced soon after he had deliberately set his course for Jerusalem, that 'the Son of man did not come to be served but to serve, and to give his life as a ransom for many.' There is little doubt that 'many' is here, following a Semitic idiom, equivalent to 'all'; equally, while the symbolism is not directly that of sacrifice but of compensation paid, the sacrificial atmosphere and implications are inescapable. In the view of most commentators the immediate background of the statement is Isaiah's portrait (53: 2–12) of the Servant of the Lord who 'makes himself an offering for sin,' who 'bore the sin of many and made intercession for the transgressors.' The connection has almost certainly been exaggerated, but it remains probable that the Servant passage has exercised at any rate an indirect influence on the logion. As Bishop A. E. J. Rawlinson once observed, 'The phrase sums up the general thought of Isaiah 53, and expresses the idea of a vicarious and voluntary giving of life, with the thought also implied that the sacrifice was in some way mysteriously necessitated by sin.'

This passage can hardly be dissociated from the report which St. Mark gives a little later (14: 22–5) of the institution of the eucharist. As he describes it, this took place as the Lord and his disciples were holding their passover celebration, that is, the annual ceremonial meal in commemoration of God's deliverance of his people at the Exodus. The significant moment comes when, as they are eating, Jesus identifies the bread which he has broken and distributed as his body, and the wine over which he has given thanks as 'my blood of the covenant, which is poured out for many.' The implication of these latter words is that the death which he is shortly to undergo is a sacrificial one, a shedding of his blood which will inaugurate a new covenant between God and man and which will have the effect of making propitiation for the sins of the people.

Both speaker and listeners, it seems likely, had before their minds the narrative of Exodus 24: 8, which relates how 'Moses took the blood [of the sacrificial victims] and threw it upon the people, and said, "Behold the blood of the covenant which the Lord has made with you".' This blood, according to ancient Jewish interpretations, had atoning power. They must also have been recalling Jeremiah's prophecy (31: 31–4) that God intended to establish a new and spiritual covenant, founded on the forgiveness of sins and resulting in perfect fellowship between himself and his people. Thus Christ's meaning, as the Evangelist would seem to have understood it, is that, just as the original covenant was ratified by blood, so his own death will be the means of bringing in a new covenant, and with it a new and blessed relationship with God; and that by partaking of the eucharistic bread and wine his disciples, and all succeeding generations of believers until the end of time, will be able to enjoy the benefits which flow from it.

(iii)

In the Pauline letters, too, the sacrificial aspect of Christ's passion is, on the surface at any rate, prominent. Among the elements of primitive tradition which the Apostle had assimilated were the dogmas that 'Christ died for our sins' (1 Cor. 15: 3), and that he 'was put to death because of our trespasses and raised for our justification' (Rom. 4: 25); and that he understood the death as sacrificial in character and effect is confirmed by his numerous references to Christ's blood as the means by which reconciliation is secured. We think, for example, of his declaration (Rom. 3: 25) that 'God put Christ forward to procure expiation by his blood, to be appropriated by faith,' as also of his remarkable statement (Rom. 5: 8–9) that 'God discloses his love for us in that, while we were still sinners, Christ died for us,' with the result that 'we are now justified by his blood.' So too he reminds the Ephesian Christians (Eph. 1: 7) that 'we have redemption through his blood, even the forgiveness of our sins,' and again (Eph. 2: 13) that, although before their conversion they had been far removed from God, they have now 'been brought near by the blood of Christ.' It was 'through the blood of his cross,' he affirms (Col. 1: 20), that reconciliation was effected between God and the rebellious universe.

The sacrificial concept is made more explicit, and at the same time given a different slant, in the claim (1 Cor. 5: 7) that 'Christ, our paschal lamb, has been sacrificed'; his is the sacrifice which ratifies the new and glorious deliverance of God's people. Similarly, in St. Paul's account of the Last Supper (1 Cor. 11: 23–6), it is its aspect as the inauguration of a new covenant that is to the fore, and the death of Jesus is viewed as the sacrifice by which this is accomplished. Most vivid and colourful of all is the affirmation in Ephesians 5: 2 that 'Christ loved us and gave himself up for us, as a fragrant offering and sacrifice to God.'

It is undeniable, therefore, that St. Paul employed sacrificial language and concepts in striving to convey the significance of Christ's passion. Some contemporary scholars have sought to play their influence down, but it seems clear that for him, with his Jewish upbringing, 'the blood of Christ' must have carried a richly sacrificial connotation; it must have suggested, by no means exclusively but assuredly in some degree, the offering up of life so that men may be reunited with God. Yet it seems equally apparent, both from the relative sparseness of unambiguously sacrificial expressions and from his readiness to pursue other lines of thought, that he did not regard this as the only or the most revealing clue to the passion. Certainly he nowhere presents an articulated theory of Christ's death as a sacrifice, nor do we find him pressing the detail of his sacrificial figures.

A good illustration of the generality of his treatment is the famous passage from Romans 3: 25 which was quoted above. While it is likely that the ritual of the Day of Atonement was present in his thoughts when he penned it, it should not be read as suggesting that God put Christ forward (as the

Authorized and Revised Versions both imply) as an actual propitiation, that is, as an offering by means of which the Father might be appeased and his righteous wrath deflected. Rather, as recent studies of the Apostle's language have shown, his argument is the more general one that Christ's death has an expiatory effect: it is a means by which sin is forgiven. Even this entails a more precise definition than he normally attempts, and we may suspect that there were at least two reasons which caused him to be chary about exploiting the symbolism of sacrifice too literally (a third will be indicated later). First, in his thinking the death of Jesus tends to be inseparably connected with his resurrection, and there were obvious difficulties in integrating this with the traditional sacrificial model. Secondly, however, it was characteristic of him to view Christ's saving action as a manifestation of God's grace rather than, as the strict use of the sacrificial category would demand, as directed towards God. From beginning to end it was a case, not of God's wrath being mollified by an acceptable victim, but of God 'in Christ reconciling the world to himself' (2 Cor. 5: 19).

(iv)

Two New Testament books which sponsor the sacrificial interpretation of the passion more wholeheartedly, though along different lines and at very different levels of sophistication, are the First Epistle of Peter and the Epistle to the Hebrews. The author of the former writes as a pastor rather than an original or constructive theologian; he is weaving into his exhortation strands of traditional teaching, often in the form of liturgical or credal excerpts. His very first sentence, with its mention (1: 2) of 'sprinkling with his blood,' recalls the expiatory sacrifices of the Old Testament and in particular those which, according to Exodus 24: 5–8, Moses offered in ratification of the covenant at Sinai; it is by the offering of Christ's blood, he implies, that the new people of God is constituted. A few lines down (1: 19) he refers again to 'the precious blood of Christ' as the price by which his readers have been ransomed from their former pagan way of life, and likens him to 'a lamb without blemish or spot.' Becoming more explicit, he declares (2: 21–4) that Christ suffered for us, that sinless though he was 'he himself bore our sins in his body on the tree,' and that 'by his wounds' we 'have been healed.' Moreover, the purpose for which Christ suffered for our sins was (3: 18) 'that he might bring us to God.' To a large extent his thinking and language are inspired by the figure of Isaiah's Servant of the Lord, who 'bore the sin of many' (Is. 53: 12) and in whose patient self-offering he sees the Redeemer foreshadowed. But other images too, such as the passover lamb and the scapegoat of the Day of Atonement ritual (Lev. 16), are all intermingled in his sketch.

The sacrificial theory presupposed in the Epistle to the Hebrews is much more thoroughly worked out, and is directly related to the cultic system of the Old Testament. Perhaps its most original and striking feature is its portrayal of Christ as at once the perfect high priest and the perfect offering. His priesthood is immeasurably superior to ordinary priesthood, first, because while sinless himself he has shared every human temptation and so can sympathize fully with human frailty (4: 15–16); secondly, because God has appointed him to a unique priesthood far more exalted than the Aaronic one (5: 5–6; 7: 1–28); thirdly, because he does not exercise it day by day in a man-made temple, but eternally in the heavens (7: 24; 10: 11–12). In harmony with this the sacrifice he offered surpassed and superseded the old Levitical sacrifices. Whereas they are repeated daily, his is 'once for all' (10: 11–12); and whereas they can never completely efface sin (10: 4), his is perfectly and finally effective (10: 12–14). And its essence is 'the blood of Christ, who through his eternal spirit offered himself without blemish to God' (9: 14). It was 'through his own blood' that 'he entered in once for all into the holy place, having obtained eternal redemption' (9: 12).

The whole object of his being crucified outside Jerusalem was that he might 'sanctify the people through his own blood' (13: 12). It is 'through the offering of the body of Jesus Christ once for all' in obedience to God's will that 'we have been sanctified' (10: 10).

The writer's thought may seem difficult to unravel, but this last sentence enables us to glimpse something of his meaning In the preceding verse, we should notice, he had appealed to Psalm 40: 6–8, which in the Greek translation he used indicates that the Psalmist perceived that animal sacrifices were of no avail to establish fellowship between man and God, but that there was a sacrifice which God did indeed will for this purpose, namely the voluntary offering up of a body, or life, he had given. This he applies to Jesus, putting into his mouth the Psalmist's prophetic words, 'Lo, I have come to do thy will.' Thus it is in his perfect fulfilment of God's redemptive will, by laying down his life on the cross, that his sacrifice consists. As a result of this fulfilment purification of sins is accomplished (1: 3), eternal redemption is procured (9: 12), men's consciences are cleansed so that they are able to serve the living God (9: 14), 'a new and living way' has been opened to the world of eternal realities (10: 20), and the new and better covenant foreseen long ago by Jeremiah has been inaugurated (7: 22; 8: 6; etc.).

(v)

A point which even this brief survey brings out is that, while freely availing themselves of the model of sacrifice, the New Testament writers nowhere provide any rationale of it. They do not employ it in a strictly literal sense, but rather as a ready-to-hand analogy to help them to express what Christ's passion has achieved. This is entirely understandable. In the Judaism in which they had grown up the true significance of sacrifice, as a result of the criticism of the prophets and others, was no longer being found in the rituals themselves but in the deeper moral and spiritual realities of which they might be the vehicles. What commended a man to God, the more reflective and spiritually alert Jewish thinkers had come to perceive, was not any gift, however precious, that he might lay on the altar, nor even any formally correct pattern of behaviour that he might assume. Rather it was a broken and contrite heart, genuine repentance, and the sincere resolve to conduct himself mercifully. What God demands is the voluntary, humble consecration of the man himself to his service. If the outward forms of sacrifice continued to be observed and held in honour (as they were bound to be, since God was believed to have ordained them), it was recognized that whatever value they possessed lay in the spirit of abasement and self-surrender of which, rightly used, they could be the expression.

Nevertheless, as it is employed by the New Testament writers, the sacrificial category does reflect another and equally profound intuition at which, under God's guidance (as we must believe), later Judaism had arrived. This was the realization that costly suffering voluntarily and humbly endured, above all the costly suffering of the righteous, possesses atoning power, and can thus be beneficial to others than the sufferer himself. We can see this conviction taking shape in the marvellous portrait of the Servant of the Lord which is set out in Isaiah's fifty-third chapter and in which, as we have more than once observed, the early Christians saw Christ's own passion and vindication prefigured. The cruel experiences which the Jewish people were called upon to undergo in the days of the Maccabees, when the nation was heroically defending its ancestral religion and way of life against powerful pagan oppressors, greatly fostered the growth and enrichment of this idea. A typical illustration is a famous passage in the Fourth Book of Maccabees (17: 22), where we read that the martyred saints have become 'a ransom for our nation's sin,' and that 'through the blood of these righteous men and their propitiatory death Divine Providence has delivered sorely afflicted Israel.' Judaism had merely glimpsed this conception, with all its far-reaching implications, as men momentarily glimpse a hidden object when a light flashes out in the darkness. For these early Christians the glimpse had become a sharply defined and assured vision because the Lord himself, in whom they believed the will and purpose of God were embodied, had endorsed it.

To twentieth-century man this inspired vision is bound at first to seem a wild surmise, a piece of extravagant optimism or perhaps even wishful thinking. We can see that suffering willingly and meekly accepted has, in a limited degree, something of a sacrificial character. It can exert a cleansing influence on the victim himself, and it can act as an example and challenge to others; in these and similar ways it can make the world a better place. But how can the martyrdom two thousand years ago of a single man, however good and holy, serve not only to encourage others to behave in similar fashion, but also provide expiation for the sins of mankind and repair their broken fellowship with God? As we have hinted, the key to the mystery, as the New Testament writers saw it, lay in their firm belief that Jesus of Nazareth was by no means just a righteous man, but God's agent and representative, indeed 'the effulgence of his glory and the very image of his being' (Heb. 1: 3). His passion could have, and in actual fact eternally has, this saving effect because it gave expression to the saving will of God.

It is here that faith discerns the objective aspect of the cross. The passion does not merely disclose God's love and patience and compassion. It does that, of course, and we shall be treating this theme later in this book. But in addition it reveals God taking the initiative, and delivering himself into the hands of men so that, by his suffering and humble acceptance, the evil in them and in the world may be overcome. And the blessed effects of this saving action extend, potentially if not actually, to the entire human race because, at a deeper level than their fragmented individuality, all men and women form a unity with one another. What affects one can be transmitted to all because this potential unity can become a reality through their entering into fellowship with Christ their brother. So understood the passion transcends the sacrificial categories in which the first Christians were inevitably driven to formulate it, and at the same time restates in more personal terms the objective victory over evil which the more imaginative pictures of Christ's conquest of Satan and the powers of darkness are seeking to convey.

5

OBEDIENCE

(i)

YET another aspect of Christ's passion to which the New Testament writers devote their attention is its character as an exhibition of obedience. The special interest of this is that it introduces us to the deeper motivation of the Redeemer. If the category of sacrifice is external and objective, stressing the removal of the barrier which keeps man from God, that of obedience is interior and subjective, with its emphasis on complete dedication to and identification with the Father's will. As such obedience and sacrifice can be viewed as complementary; the one supplies the spiritual basis and substance of the other.

In approaching this aspect it is useful to remember that obedience is a key-concept in the Old Testament as in the Bible as a whole. The background of our discussion should be the realization that centuries before Jesus lived and died Judaism was profoundly aware of its supreme importance for religion. The best of Hebrew prophecy had perceived that without obedience sacrifice itself is a mockery, and we have an excellent illustration of this in Samuel's famous declaration (1 Sam. 15: 22), 'Behold, to obey is better than sacrifice, and to hearken than the fat of rams.' The reason underlying this is that, in the Bible way of looking at things, obedience is the indispensable element in the attitude of the creature to the Creator. Conceiving of God in personal, not metaphysical, terms, the Bible logically visualizes the harmony and proper ordering of reality by the analogy of personal relations. Thus in the Adam story the essence of sin, and of man's tragic alienation from his Maker, is located in disobedience and self-assertion; and God's revelation of himself in the Old Testament is dominated by the idea of a covenant setting before his people a pattern of life which they are morally obliged to observe.

(ii)

Not surprisingly, therefore, obedience is one of the strands woven into the complex texture of the New Testament interpretation of the passion. In the Synoptic Gospels this facet is more often implied than overtly stated. It underlies, for example, their repeated insistence that suffering and death are a divine necessity laid upon Jesus, and one that he voluntarily accepts, with full foreknowledge of what is coming to him, because he knows that it is his Father's will. Earlier in their narrative it is hinted at in the story of the Temptations in the wilderness. Faced with the choice between the claims of God and worldly success, Jesus unhesitatingly elects to serve God, although he is already aware what the cost is going to be. Occasionally, however, this motive is brought right into the foreground. Thus there is no scene in the Gospels more sombrely impressive than St. Mark's picture (10: 32) of Jesus striding ahead of the 'amazed' disciples as they set out for Jerusalem. He knows full well that the cross awaits him, but nothing can quench his determination to do what is demanded of him.

Even more eloquent and moving, however, is the description of his agony in the Garden of Gethsemane. In all three accounts (Matthew 26: 36–46; Mark 14: 32–42; Luke 22: 41–6) the Saviour passes through a period of severe mental distress and anguish, even praying that he may not have to drink the bitter cup. But his authentic resolve is disclosed, in all its simple and unfaltering dignity, when he exclaims at the climax, 'Nevertheless, not as I will, but as thou wilt.'

In the Fourth Gospel the idea of obedience to, and entire dependence on, the Father's will is the foundation upon which St. John builds up his own special theory of the passion, the main lines of which we shall be studying later. In his view Jesus is the revealer of the one true God, inseparably united with him (10: 30) and reflecting his character so faithfully that to see the incarnate Lord is to see the Father (14: 9). And the token of this profound unity is that throughout he acts in conformity with the Father's will, invariably and with complete docility reproducing in his own actions what he sees the Father do (5: 19–20). As he declares (5: 30), 'I do not seek my own will, but the will of him who sent me'; and again (6: 38), 'I have not come down from heaven to do my own will, but the will of him who sent me.' When he is hungry and his disciples invite him to eat, he enigmatically replies (4: 31–4) that he has food of his own of which they are ignorant, and then explains, 'My food is to do the will of him who sent me, and to accomplish his work.'

As the narrative proceeds, it becomes clear that this allotted task which he thus obediently undertakes reaches its climax in suffering and death. It is to these that he 'consecrates' himself (17: 19), and by these that, when the supreme hour has come (17: 1), he knows that both he will glorify God and God him. It is by submitting to death that he accomplishes the work which God has given him to do (17: 4); and when death finally comes to the Crucified, he can bow his head and say (19: 30), 'It is finished.' This single, expressive verb (one word in the original Greek) should not be taken simply as announcing that his last moment has arrived, but rather as giving voice to his realization that the task he has obediently shouldered has now been completed.

(iii)

Obedience and submissiveness to God's will are also key-ideas in the First Epistle of Peter. The writer expects (1: 14) his readers, Christians as they are, to be 'obedient children,' and requires (2: 13–3: 7) the different groups in the Asian communities to which he is writing to show appropriate sub-

servience to each other. The example he holds up to them
(2: 21-3) is Christ himself, who in his passion displayed in-
finite patience and committed himself unreservedly to God. In
agreement with this he regularly envisages faith, or its opposite, as obeying, or disobeying, the gospel (e.g. 1: 22; 2: 8).

But the part played by obedience in Christ's saving work
is more vividly highlighted in the Epistle to the Hebrews. As
we saw in the last chapter, the concept which primarily deter-
mines its author's approach to the passion is sacrifice; this is
the once-for-all and perfect sacrifice to which ancient prophecy pointed and which God wished to be made. But the
essential element in it, as he understands the transaction, is
Christ's offering of himself for men in complete obedience to
the will of God. When he contrasts Christ's sacrifice with the
traditional sacrifices of Israel and seeks to identify what gives
it superior, indeed surpassing worth, it is precisely this, as we
noticed, that he picks on (10: 5-9): 'Lo, I am come to do thy
will.' So it is through this dedicated will, he emphasizes
(10: 10), that 'we have been sanctified as the result of the
offering of the body of Jesus Christ once for all.' We over-
simplify and distort his meaning, however, if we suppose it to
be that what God requires of men is perfect moral obedience
in contrast to external sacrifices, and that the work of Christ
consists in uniquely exhibiting such obedience and thereby
attaining moral perfection. Rather (as we saw) his thought is
that, in his longing to bring men back into fellowship with
himself (2: 10), God does indeed require a sacrifice, but such
a sacrifice as that which the obedient surrender of his life by
Christ could alone provide. When he entered the world, Jesus
was fully conscious of this and thus, 'though he was a Son,
yet he learned obedience by the things he suffered' (5: 8); thus
God's redemptive will has been fulfilled because in his passion
the Lord identified himself obediently with it, being made
'perfect through suffering' (2: 10).

(iv)

As we see, the sacrificial category is still paramount in the
Epistle to the Hebrews; while convinced that Christ's obedient
acceptance of God's will makes his the supreme sacrifice, the
writer nowhere answers the question how it achieves its
results. For a more thorough analysis of Christ's passion and
death in terms of obedience, we should turn to St. Paul. He is
ready enough, as we noted in the previous chapter, to apply
the symbolism of sacrifice to them, but this is not the deepest
or most characteristic element in his thinking. The verb 'obey'
and its cognates occur much more frequently in his letters
than in all the remaining books of the New Testament taken
together, and it is arguable that his primary understanding of
the death of Jesus is as an expression of his obedience. For
this insight it is obvious that he was deeply indebted to his
Jewish inheritance. For Judaism the supreme duty, as also the
highest joy, of God's chosen people was to offer him unswerving, sincerely felt obedience; and the best Jewish thought
of St. Paul's time looked upon the martyrdom of the man who
suffered in God's service as the crowning manifestation of this.
Educated himself as a rabbi and starting from premises like
these, the Apostle was able to combine them with his own
exalted conception of Christ's person and reach forward to a
richer appreciation both of the inner significance of his passion
and of what it achieves for mankind.

Two famous passages are particularly instructive. The first
is Philippians 2: 3–11, which starts off as a warmly pastoral
exhortation to his readers to be like-minded, mutually affectionate and, above all, entirely unselfish and humble. Then,
with a sudden change of tone, it points them to Christ as their
model, and in a series of hymn-like strophes eloquently
sketches his mission, seizing on his obedience as its crucial
trait. Although he had pre-existed 'in the form of God,' he
had not counted this something to be grasped hold of, but had
abandoned divine status and consented to enter into the

human condition and to be born as a man, thus 'taking the form of a servant.' More than that, he 'humbled himself and became obedient unto death, even death on a cross.' Absolute obedience therefore was the inward motivation of his passion, and it was to crown his self-sacrificial obedience that God at his resurrection 'highly exalted him' and assigned him the supreme title of 'Lord.' It is as the One who, unique in his self-humbling (who has ever, like him, exchanged 'the form of God' for 'the form of a servant'?), has been unique also in his obedience unto death that he has now been empowered to exercise his lordship over the whole realm of creation.

Our second passage is the well-known one in Romans 5: 17–19, in which St. Paul contrasts the obedience of Christ with the disobedience of Adam, and is thus able to indicate how the beneficial effects of the passion can extend to all mankind. Earlier on he has recalled (5: 6) that 'while we were still helpless, at the right time, Christ died for the ungodly,' and has claimed (5: 1) that as a result 'we have peace with God through our Lord Jesus Christ.' The disordered state of the human race (so runs his argument), which finds its existential manifestation in man's separation from God, is the direct product of its disobedience, and this is traceable to the defiance which Adam, its first ancestor and representative, exhibited to God's express command. This rebellion, with its appalling consequences of sin, enmity with God and death, extended to all his descendants, and is the condition of what we should call the natural man. But with the coming of Christ the ancient disastrous legacy has been broken, and a new family of human beings enjoying peace and fellowship with their Maker has been brought into existence. And this has been made possible precisely because Christ, the representative man, by accepting the cross and going to his death, reversed Adam's primordial defiance and instead submitted himself unreservedly to the divine will. Thus (5: 19), 'as by one man's disobedience many were made sinners, so by one man's obedience many will be made righteous.' The great difference, not stated but clearly

implied, is that whereas Adam's disobedience and the penalty
it incurred are transmitted to his posterity by natural generation, the new family of Christ which has been reconciled by
his obedience is constituted by their free acceptance of the
gospel by faith.

(v)

The interpretation of the passion in terms of obedience is
much more immediately congenial to modern habits of thinking than, say, sacrifice. St. Paul's analysis, it will be observed,
goes deeper and is more far-reaching than those of the other
New Testament writers. For the author of Hebrews, for example, Christ's obedience is his ready identification of himself
with the Father's redeeming will. The Apostle, however,
understands it much more widely as his total acceptance of,
and submission to, whatever God decrees. Christ's attitude, as
he sees it, is thus exactly the opposite of Adam's, and in so
far as men and women align themselves with it they form a
group which is orientated entirely differently from that which
follows Adam's example.

An initial difficulty, of course, for contemporary Christians
concerns the historical Adam. Few, if any, of us are likely to
share St. Paul's assumption that Genesis 1–3 is the record of
events which actually happened. Yet the recognition that the
Adam story is myth should be no bar to our acknowledging
the profound truth which it encloses. There is a deep-seated
disorder in human existence, whether studied in the individual
or in the community, which prevents it from attaining authentic fulfilment. Present-day humanism hotly denies this; but its
complacency and optimism seem curiously parochial when
compared with the more realistic appraisal offered not only
by Christianity, but by keen-eyed philosophers like Martin
Heidegger and J. P. Sartre, penetrating students of human
nature like Hobbes and Freud, and a whole line of poets,
dramatists and novelists without any specifically religious

allegiance. And if we adopt the religious stance, believing in a God who has created men as free agents and who has designed a particular destiny for them, it is by no means implausible that the root of this disorder should be something which can be fairly described as disobedience, the wilfully obstinate refusal of the creature to conform to the Creator's purposes. If this be the situation, then the radical frustration, the sense of alienation and lostness of which most sensitive men and women, left to themselves, are acutely conscious, and which everywhere finds an explosive outlet in the disorders of society, finds a persuasive explanation.

Set in this context, the New Testament interpretation of Christ's passion as an act of supreme obedience throws precious light on the solution of the human predicament. According to St. Paul's teaching, there is a solidarity between all members of the human race which he attributes to their common descent from Adam, and as a result of which they are all implicated in the radical disobedience which he initiated. Both liberal Christianity and secular humanism, with their exaltation of the individual as an isolated existent, have tended to look with suspicion on the notion of solidarity; but recent studies of the origins and development of man, of primitive folklore and mythology, of the subconscious, racial memory and group psychology, and of sociology should have supplied a healthy corrective to atomic individualism. It seems obvious that, if from one aspect man is complete in himself, from another he is a member of, and profoundly influenced by, the wider social community. This impinges on him, even before he is born, at levels far below his consciousness; and since it is itself the product of forces stretching far back in history, it is understandable that it should be the means of involving him in the frustration and rebellion which characterize the race as such.

Similarly, as the New Testament views it, Christ's obedience is not simply one man's glorious achievement, a dazzling reminder to human beings of what God expects of them and a challenge to imitation. Although he comes from God, bringing the divine grace and power into the world of men, he is himself authentically man, sharing with us the human experience in all its fullness and depth, and as such is the new Adam, the pioneer of a new race. There is a solidarity between him and those who adhere to him by faith analogous to, and though different in kind as rich in impact as, the solidarity between the first Adam and his physical descendants. Thus the obedience which marked his whole life, and which he supremely exhibited in his passion, has decisively altered the whole human situation. Against the defiance of God, and consequent alienation from him, which have prevailed hitherto, is set the new obedience, with peace and reconciliation as its crown. 'For as in Adam all die, so also in Christ shall all be made alive' (1 Cor. 15: 22).

6

THE LOVE OF GOD

(i)

WHENEVER Christians have reflected on the passion, they have felt drawn to interpret it as a revelation of God's love for mankind. They have taken to their hearts a famous statement of St. Augustine's, which appears in a handbook he compiled for the instruction of catechumens: 'The chief cause of Christ's coming was that men might learn how much God loves them.' The New Testament writers would not have subscribed to that sentence exactly as it stands; the object of the incarnation, as they saw it, was not so much to disclose a wonderful truth about God's nature and attitude as to accomplish a saving work. Nevertheless they freely and gratefully acknowledged that the motivating force behind the redemptive action was the divine love, and that at every stage in Christ's ministry, and most eloquently and vividly in his passion, that love was being made visible for those with eyes to see.

The idea of God as a loving God, as loving at any rate his chosen people, was of course familiar to them from the Old Testament, which depicts God's relation with Israel as an intensely personal one. This awareness of a special relationship must have come to birth in the experience of the Exodus, that formative turning-point in Israel's history when the nation had had direct and convincing proof of God's loving care for it. It was the prophets, however, whose inspired insight elaborated it in rich and often poignant imagery. Jeremiah, for example, makes much of the suffering love of God, representing him (12: 7–9) as abandoning his rebellious people but still cherishing it as 'the beloved of my soul,' and in a later passage (31: 20) as moved with tenderness whenever he thinks

55

of Ephraim, 'my dear son . . . my darling child.' Hosea in particular, drawing on the tragedy of his own domestic life, finds himself (3: 1) catching a glimpse of God's compassionate love for faithless, backsliding Israel in his own yearning for the adulterous wife who has betrayed him. Varying his metaphor, he pictures God as a fond father teaching his child to walk, leading Ephraim 'with cords of love' despite its heedlessness to his call and guidance (11: 1–4). Indeed the divine love is for him (11: 9) far superior to human love, since it refuses to be swayed even by righteous anger and is rooted in the mystery of God's being.

(ii)

With their minds steeped in this inheritance, the New Testament writers might have been expected to interpret Christ's work as illustrating the forgiving love of God in action. On a hasty reading, however, one is tempted to conclude that the first three Evangelists at any rate were slow to read this meaning into it; what chiefly impresses them, as we saw in Chapter II, is its mysterious necessity. No doubt the explanation of this largely lies in the fact that, until they had pondered its significance more deeply, their immediate reaction was bound to be puzzlement and shock at the Messiah's ignominious death. Nevertheless, while the passion seemed to them a mysterious necessity, it was a necessity which was grounded in the purpose of God. Moreover, as they envisage it, this divine purpose had as its objective the overcoming of evil, the expiation of human sin, the reconciliation of men with God, and the inauguration of a new covenant relationship. Thus if the love of God is nowhere brought into the open in the Synoptic accounts of the passion, it overshadows them, obscurely but pervasively, as the determining motive.

This becomes clear when we examine the portrait of God which they consistently present, and which is itself inspired by the teaching of Jesus. This portrait shows us a merciful and forgiving Father, who expects us to go to any lengths to for-give each other, even those who insult us and are wickedly disposed towards us, because that is how he behaves towards us. If we need to be convinced of this, we have only to make a careful study of such a passage as the fifteenth chapter of St. Luke's Gospel. This starts by describing the intense annoy-ance of the Scribes and Pharisees because of Christ's readi-ness to offer hospitality to 'tax-collectors and sinners' (that is, pagans and not good Jews), classes of persons normally reckoned to be outside the pale. Then it sets down the three graphic stories by telling which Jesus, in his characteristic manner, reduced them to abashed silence. The first centres on the comfortably off farmer who, although possessing a hundred sheep in his flock, would not dream of sparing any effort to retrieve the single sheep which had got lost. The second describes the excitement and joy of the prudent house-wife who, after turning the house upside down, at last finds the one and only coin she has lost from her little hoard. The third is about the spendthrift and dissipated young man who eventually comes to his senses and creeps timidly home, down-cast and ashamed, only to discover that his father not only loves him with undiminished affection but is preparing an un-precedented feast to celebrate his return. These are homely tales from everyday life; but when the Evangelist recorded them, he was aware that what they were really intended to illustrate was the boundless concern and love which God him-self has for men and women who go astray, his surpassing joy when they find their way back to him, and the extraordinary lengths he is prepared to go, even to the extent of sending his Son to die on the cross, in order to secure their return.

(iii)

For all their apparent reticence, therefore, it is evident that the Synoptic writers, understanding the passion as they did as the fulfilment of divine purpose, must have discerned in it the operation and splendid expression of God's concern and love for men. There is no corresponding reticence in St. Paul, as becomes crystal clear if we examine for a moment his powerful argument in the closing paragraph of the eighth chapter of Romans. The Apostle is describing, in a series of boldly rhetorical questions, the splendour of the new age which has been ushered in by Christ's death and resurrection, and his exhortation can be compared to an elaborately constructed symphony with three interlocking movements. Its starting-point (8: 28) is the love which God's chosen people, or the elect, have for him; it advances (8: 35) to the love of Christ; and its finale (8: 39) is the confident assurance that we can never be separated 'from the love of God which is in Christ Jesus our Lord.'

The foundation facts on which this assurance is based are three. The first is that, as the whole of St. Paul's experience of the gospel has demonstrated, God has called him, and both justifies and glorifies those whom he has called; God is therefore 'on our side' or 'for us' (8: 28–31). The second is that, as a token of his being 'on our side,' God has allowed his Son to become man (8: 3)—the Son whom the Apostle elsewhere (Col. 1: 13) calls 'the Son of his love'—and furthermore 'did not spare his own Son but has given him up for us all' (8: 32). Thus God's movement of love and condescension found its fitting expression in the voluntary death of the Son 'who loved us' (8: 37), and who is now at his Father's right hand interceding for us (8: 34). Thirdly, as St. Paul has already announced in a previous chapter (5: 5), a new life has been initiated for believers by these saving events, 'because God's love has been poured into our hearts through the Holy Spirit which has been given to us.' It is the presence of the Spirit which ensures that we can never be cut off from God's love.

Though the argument needs some disentangling, the passage makes it plain that for the Apostle the divine love is the driving force in the work of Christ. Earlier in the same Epistle (5: 8) he had made the point in a single, blindingly translucent sentence: 'God shows his love for us in that while we were still sinners Christ died for us.' What he means is not simply that the passion is an illustration of God's love, or a symbol of it, but that God's love was actually operative in it. In closely similar terms, in the Epistle to the Ephesians, after describing the moral death and shameful subjection to desire which dominated his correspondents before their conversion, he explains (2: 1–6) that their whole situation has been amazingly transformed as a result of Christ's death and resurrection; and this transformation has come about because God 'is rich in mercy' and because 'of the great love with which he loved us.'

God's love is not mentioned directly in the Epistle to the Galatians, but it is the underlying presupposition of its whole great argument. The gist of this is that ever since Abraham's day God has been planning the creation of a people free from the domination of the Law, who in the fullest sense of the word are his adoptive sons and can therefore address him as 'Father'; and that he has achieved this by sending his Son, by allowing him to be crucified in obedience to the Law's demands, and, finally, by bestowing on them the Spirit which is seen to be the Spirit of love. This is the gospel of the cross and resurrection of Jesus Christ which St. Paul claims to have preached to the Galatians and from which he is distressed to hear that they are deviating; and as they read the letter, they must have realized that the good news it contained was the proclamation of God's love in action.

(iv)

For all their profound difference of theological standpoint, St. John is at one with St. Paul in discerning the love of God behind the incarnation, passion and resurrection of Christ. A passage in his Gospel which we should consider in this connection is the first half (verses 1–21) of the third chapter. This relates the conversation which Jesus held with Nicodemus when that 'ruler of the Jews' visited him by night and they talked about the possibility of a man's seeing, or entering into, God's kingdom. Jesus explains that this goal cannot be reached either by learned discussions such as the one in which he and Nicodemus are engaged, or by miraculous signs of the kind Nicodemus has been complimenting him on, but only by undergoing a complete spiritual renewal. Indeed, the favoured man must be born afresh of water and the Spirit, and for this it is necessary that Jesus, the Son of man who has descended from heaven and has thereby bridged heaven and earth, should be 'lifted up' and again ascend to heaven. In less veiled language, the new order which is God's kingdom is brought into being through the passion, death and resurrection of the Lord himself. And the reason for this, the Evangelist interpolates (3: 16), is to be sought for in the love of God: it was precisely because God had such a love for the world that he gave his Son to suffer and die and rise again. The object at which God's love is directed is men's salvation, that they may attain eternal life; but this love only becomes effective in so far as men believe in Christ—otherwise it turns, reluctantly but inevitably, to judgment.

In St. John's theology particular emphasis is placed (see, for example, 3: 35 and 10: 17) on the love of the Father for the Son, and he conceives of the Son's function as being to mediate that love to men. It is this supreme love which he is manifesting when he lays down his life for his friends (15: 13); and when the hour of his passion approaches, St. John describes Jesus (13: 1) as having loved his own in the world and as now loving them 'to the end.' This last expression contains two layers of meaning, suggesting at once the absoluteness and completeness of the Saviour's love, and also that it continued undiminished till, and was exhibited at, the final moment of his life.

A few paragraphs later in the same thirteenth chapter, after Jesus has washed his disciples' feet and supped with them and watched Judas go out on his treacherous mission, St. John describes (13:34) how he gave them his 'new commandment' and told them that they should love one another 'just as I have loved you.' The immediate reference of these words is, of course, to the affectionate, self-effacing service he has done them in washing their feet, but the feet-washing itself is clearly a figurative pointer to the infinitely greater service he is going to perform by his dying. But all this love of his is a passing on to those whom he calls his friends (his disciples in the first instance, but also his followers in every age) of the love of God, with whom, as the Evangelist emphasizes (for example, 10:30—'I and my Father are one') he is inseparably united and whose essence in fact is love (1 John 4:8). A point which St. John presses home is that the Father loves the Son precisely because he lays down his life for men (10:17). What he is suggesting is not that the Father loves Christ because he was crucified, but that in the crucifixion the Father's own love is disclosed. As he indicates elsewhere (17:22–6), God's love reaches the world of men through the Son's self-giving, and by what the Son has done and is they can know that the Father loves them with a love no whit less than the love he has for him.

Exactly the same thought is echoed, in simpler and more straightforward language, in St. John's First Epistle. There we read (4:7–21) that God's love should be the pattern and main-spring of our love for one another. As he puts it, the man who does not love clearly lacks all knowledge of God and is cut off from him, because God himself is love. And both the fact that God loves us and the character of his love have been laid bare in the passion, because God sent his unique and uniquely loved Son so that human beings might have life through him. He not only sent him into our sin-stained world, but sent him 'to be the expiation for our sins,' that is, to suffer and die so that, through his sacrificial act, our sins might obtain the divine forgiveness. As a result, St. John assures his readers (4:17–19), even in the hour of judgment believers can

approach God with love themselves, discarding the awful
dread which the natural man is bound to feel in the presence
of the Holy One, because God has himself taken the initiative
in loving them.

(v)

There is no need to dwell at length on the transformation of
our ordinary view of life which the acceptance of the passion
as the revelation of God's love entails. Most of us are liable
to be overwhelmed, in certain moods and in certain situations
at any rate, by the apparent meaningless and futility of
existence. When we contemplate the indifference and sheer
irrationality of many natural happenings, the squalid mixture
of criminality, violence and folly which seem to be the stuff
of human history, the callousness, brutal selfishness and naked
cruelty of man to man, and the tragedy which cuts across so
many individual lives, it is difficult to credit the claim that a
God of justice, much less of love, presides over the process.
The cynics who used to taunt the Psalmist (for example,
Psalm 42: 3, 10) with the mocking question, 'Where is your God
now?', and who flaunt the same jibe to-day, cannot be dis-
missed as superficial in their analysis; apart from the gospel,
their case is a plausible one. And if the gospel refutes them,
it is precisely because we are persuaded that we have in the
passion a group of historical facts, uniquely weighty and of
unique significance, which run completely counter to the
verdict of the other facts of history. This group of facts is
unique because we believe that the action of Christ in voluntarily surrendering his life on the cross was in a genuine sense
the action of God himself, and that the certification of this is
his resurrection from the dead.

In other words, our faith in the passion as the disclosure of
the divine love (as indeed our acceptance of those other wonderful aspects of the cross we have been drawing out in earlier
chapters) is grounded in, and can only be sustained by, our

faith in Christ's person. When the New Testament writers lived, they were only beginning to work out a theology of the incarnation, and Christians in that age were very far from having agreed any formal statement of it. But the conviction that God was in Christ, revealing himself in the man born of Mary and as incarnate Lord intervening decisively in human life and history, is the presupposition of all their teaching, preaching and living. And unless Christians to-day retain the substance of that conviction, whether in the classic formulation of the Church's creeds or restated in fresh categories more congenial to their thinking, their optimism must amount to little more than sentimentality and romanticism.

Two further points should perhaps be added so as to clarify the New Testament understanding of God as love and the implications which flow from it. First, there has been a tendency among theologians to distinguish sharply between divine love and human love. For human beings, they argue, love even at its best is always fundamentally self-centred; they are drawn to the beloved object by the desire to possess and enjoy it, and any concern for its welfare is secondary. By contrast the divine love is characterized wholly by self-giving, and seeks nothing in return. But surely this involves an artificial and altogether unacceptable antithesis; if it corresponded with the facts, it is hard to see how two such utterly contrary attitudes could ever have had the same name applied to them. Certainly the picture we obtain of God's love in the Biblical revelation makes nonsense of the dichotomy, whether we think of Isaiah's or Jeremiah's descriptions of Yahweh's love for Israel in terms of a father's yearning for his disloyal children, or whether we reflect on the great Johannine text 'God so loved that he gave.' The inescapable inference is that God's relationship with us is entirely personal, and that he desires our love in return.

But, secondly, the recognition that God's love was manifesting itself in the death and resurrection of Jesus suggests that there is in the universe, welling up from its creative centre but calling forth a response in us, a healing, cleansing and transforming power of which we could have had no inkling apart from the gospel. Death, suffering and man-willed evil are the three enemies, invincible and assuming countless shapes, which seem to hold our race in an ineluctable grasp. Yet in the passion we see Christ confronting them, not with a show of irresistible might, but with meekness and patience, in the strength of God's love; and that love, which according to St. Paul (Rom. 5: 5) has been poured into our hearts through his Holy Spirit, prevails over them and eliminates them once for all.

7

LIFE AND GLORY

(i)

IN this chapter we shall consider two insights into the significance of the passion for which we are largely indebted to St. John. The first, that in his self-sacrifice Jesus Christ is revealed as resurrection and life, is of course not confined to the Fourth Gospel. It underlies, for example, the Pauline theology of the Christian's mystical death and resurrection in baptism; it inspires the hymn-fragment cited in 2 Timothy 2: 11, which proclaims, 'If we have died with him, we shall also live with him.' Nevertheless St. John develops it with special elaboration and in characteristic ways. The second insight, which sees in Christ's death the decisive manifestation of the divine glory, is his unique contribution. In studying both we shall be moving on a different plane of ideas than we have been traversing hitherto, but one which has been traced out by the Evangelist who, as well as pondering most deeply the meaning of the Easter happenings, has striven most strenuously to translate it into a non-Hebraic idiom.

(ii)

Every reader of the Fourth Gospel knows that one of its cardinal themes is eternal life. Indeed the Evangelist announces (20: 31) that his chief purpose in writing the book is 'that you may believe that Jesus is the Christ, the Son of God, and that believing you may have life in his name'; while in differentiating his role as the Good Shepherd from that of the destructive thief, Christ himself defines (10: 10) the object of his coming as 'that you may have life, and have it in abundance.' In the Johannine vocabulary this key-term 'life' has different shades of meaning, and sometimes they overlap. In a number of contexts it carries the accepted Jewish sense of life of the age to come, or (as we should say) the future life. An obvious and striking example is the passage (5: 28-9) in which Christ contrasts 'the resurrection of life' with 'the resurrection of judgment' which will be the lot of those who have behaved well or ill respectively. But in other contexts, more numerous and characteristic, the life which is spoken of is a blessed experience which the believer can enjoy here on earth. As Christ himself puts it in a sentence (5: 24) almost immediately preceding the one just cited, 'He who hears my word and believes on him who sent me possesses eternal life; he does not come to judgment, but has passed from death to life.' In other words, this is the divine life which, as we are taught in the prologue of the Gospel (1: 4), is in Christ and becomes the light of men.

As this passage reveals, St. John's understanding of eternal life moves consistently on two levels which he apparently regards as mutually complementary. In one breath he conceives of it as the life of the body which has been raised from the grave, that restoration of life after death which the Saviour promises to his faithful followers; in the next he envisages it as a richer, fuller dimension of existence to which faith introduces the believer while he is still alive and which makes physical death irrelevant. Both these aspects are brought together and combined in Christ's famous statement (6: 54), 'He who eats my flesh and drinks my blood possesses eternal life [that is, as an experienced actuality], and I shall raise him up at the last day.' But these two aspects, the realistic and the mystical (if this adjective is appropriate), are even more impressively juxtaposed and illustrated in the story of the Raising of Lazarus, and this we must now briefly examine.

For most of the narrative we seem to be moving on the level of physical realities. Lazarus is really dead and has been placed in his grave; his family are overwhelmed with grief, and both Martha and Mary are convinced that, if only Jesus had been there, their brother would not have died. Then the Lord, deeply moved and filled with compassion, summons the dead man, still wrapped in his grave-clothes, from the tomb, and he comes out alive again. The event is a miracle of power which, in the planning of his Gospel, the Evangelist deliberately inserts and pinpoints as anticipating the final resurrection, intending thus to give reassurance to his readers. At the same time the more spiritual conception of eternal life shines through the apparently factual story. It comes to light most strikingly when Martha has agreed that Lazarus will rise again at the final resurrection, and in reply Jesus affirms (11: 25–6), 'I am the resurrection and the life. He who believes in me will be brought to life even though he should die, and every one who is alive and has faith in me will never die.'

Both halves of this sentence deserve to be pondered. In the first half Jesus adds his endorsement to the view, accepted in contemporary Judaism except by the Sadducees, that the dead will rise again; the fresh point which he underlines is that the life-giving power which will enable them to do so issues from himself. In the second half, however, he goes beyond popular ideas about the resurrection and the possibility of life after death. He roundly asserts that the man who 'is alive and has faith in me' will be immune from death. The implication is that there is a form or dimension of life, evidently based on and stemming from commitment to Christ, which is available to us while still in the body and which is in no way impaired, much less destroyed, by the inevitable death of the body. Thus the raising of Lazarus is not merely a parable-like anticipation of the final resurrection, a dramatic reminder that faith in Christ guarantees us against the ultimate annihilation of death. It is also the symbol of a more profound and meaningful resurrection, in which through faith in Christ men and women pass to an altogether different order of existence and participate in a blessedness which neither death nor circumstance can erode.

(iii)

On a casual reading of the Fourth Gospel we might be tempted to infer that this transfigured life which Christ bestows on believers is a mystical experience, akin perhaps to that raising of the self to the timeless condition which, according to Platonic idealism, belongs to the realm of true being. That it has some affinity with this can hardly be denied, for such Hellenistic notions were widely current in the late first century and the Evangelist probably had in view an audience which was familiar with them. But to interpret his meaning exclusively, or even largely, in such terms would involve a disastrous distortion. For St. John the eternal life which Christ bestows, whether understood as the physical raising again of the dead or as the enjoyment here and now of a blessed fellowship with God, is intimately related to his passion and sacrificial act.

The attentive reader has already been given a hint of this in the chapter preceding the Raising of Lazarus. There Christ has described himself as the Good Shepherd who makes it his aim to give his followers life in abundance; and four times over in a single paragraph (10: 11, 15, 17, 18) he has emphasized his role as consisting in laying down his own life on behalf of his sheep. The Lazarus story itself is enclosed in a framework which is clearly intended to highlight its deeper significance. Its prelude is a brief but poignant conversation between Jesus and his disciples (11: 7–16), from which it emerges that the inescapable condition of his awakening Lazarus from sleep is his making the journey to Jerusalem and facing there the certain death which his enemies are preparing for him. Its sequel (11: 47–53) is the account of the hasty meeting of the Sanhedrin at which the formal decision is taken to execute Jesus. It was at this gathering, and to justify this sentence, that the high priest, speaking more truly than he knew, made his famous pronouncement (11: 50) that 'it is advantageous for you that a single man should die for the people.' The Evangelist is quick to point out to us that this was in fact a prophetic utterance, made by Caiaphas in virtue of the priestly office he was actually abusing, and that its deeper import was the gathering into one of all God's scattered children by the death of their Chief Shepherd. Thus, as St. John sees the matter, it is not by imparting new knowledge or communicating an uplifting experience, but as the result of his voluntary sacrifice of himself on the cross, that Christ brings resurrection and eternal life to men and women.

(iv)

To understand St. John's second insight, his recognition of the passion as the supreme revelation of the divine glory, we need first to recall what this term 'glory' represented in the thinking of first-century Jews brought up in a Hellenistic tradition. In the Greek Bible which they studied it is used to translate the Hebrew *kabod,* a word which signifies the manifestation of God's being, nature and presence, as these are apprehended in human experience. It is thus conceived of as the splendour of light or awesome radiance in which his power and majesty are disclosed.

In the Book of Exodus, for example, when Moses ascends Mount Sinai to receive the stone tablets inscribed with the Law, we read (24: 15–17) that 'the glory of the Lord settled on' the mountain, and that 'the appearance of the glory of the Lord was like a devouring fire.' Again, when Ezekiel by the river Chebar in Babylon has his vision (1: 4–28) of the transcendent and omnipresent God, it takes the form of a superhuman being enthroned and encompassed with a fiery brightness which he acknowledges as 'the appearance of the likeness of the glory of the Lord.' Later in the book (43: 1–5) Ezekiel recounts another vision, in which he sees the same glory of the Lord, the same dazzling brightness he had seen among the exiles in Babylon, returning to Jerusalem and entering the restored and re-designed sanctuary, so that 'the glory of the

Lord filled the temple.' In similar fashion the Psalmist pictures God as radiant light 'shining forth out of Sion' (50: 2), or as 'clothed with light as with a garment' (104: 2). In general in the Old Testament the divine glory, which fills heaven and earth alike, is God's disclosure of his being in creation and mighty acts, and the faithful look forward to its final manifestation in the messianic age.

In the New Testament the term acquires a fresh and richer connotation through being associated with the person of Christ. This is not surprising, since for the New Testament writers he is God's final and decisive Word, reflecting the glory of God and bearing the very stamp of his nature (Heb. 1: 2–3). According to St. Luke (2: 9), the glory of the Lord God had shone around the shepherds tending their flocks near Bethlehem on the night of the Saviour's birth; while St. Paul was sure (Rom. 6: 4) that 'Christ was raised from the dead by the glory of the Father.' At the Transfiguration the three privileged disciples were granted a momentary glimpse of the glory of Jesus himself.

For the most part, however, when the New Testament speaks of the glory of Christ, the reference is not to him as living on earth in human form, but as the risen and exalted Lord. It is this Risen Lord, wrapped about with dazzling brightness, whom St. Paul encounters on the road to Damascus and whose summons he feels impelled to obey (Acts 22: 6–11). St. Mark (13: 26), painting the picture of the last day, describes 'the Son of man coming in clouds with great power and glory'; and for St. Peter (1 Pet. 4: 13; cf. 5: 1) his Second Coming will be 'the revelation of his glory.' The same connection of glory with exaltation is found in St. Luke's account of the conversation of the Risen Lord with the two disciples on the road to Emmaus, in which he reminds them (24: 26) that it was necessary 'that the Christ should suffer these things and enter into his glory.' As St. Paul expresses it (Phil. 3: 21), it is as a result of the resurrection that Christ's earthly body has become his 'body of glory'; and the hope of Christians is to be glorified with their risen Saviour (Rom. 8: 17).

(v)

In the Fourth Gospel there is a significant shift of perspective. Glory is one of St. John's distinctive themes, and in his very first chapter he declares (1: 14), as representative of the apostolic Church, that 'we beheld his glory.' This is the glory of the incarnate Jesus, the glory which he has as the only-begotten Son of the Father, the glory of the Word who has been with God from everlasting (1: 1) and thus shares the divine nature. This is the glory which, as Christ himself announces later in the Gospel (17: 24), God in his great love imparted to him before the foundation of the world, and which now, in his historical person and in the actions he performs, has been brought within the apprehension of human beings.

To apprehend it, of course, they need the discernment of faith; if they lack this, their eyes are necessarily blind to the divine reality moving and operating in their midst. The miracles of Jesus, in particular, are 'signs' (a characteristic Johannine usage) by which, to those who can pierce through to the deeper truth enshrined in them, he 'manifested his glory' (2: 11). St. John here makes an advance on the other three Evangelists, for while they regard the miracles as evidences that God's kingdom is at hand, he accepts them as the actualization of God's power and presence in the world of men. Hence, when Lazarus seems fatally stricken, Jesus explains (11: 4) that his illness 'is not unto death,' that is, will not terminate in death, but has befallen him 'for the glory of God,' that is, in order that, through the sign which Jesus is about to work, the glory of God (which is also his glory) may be revealed and he himself thereby glorified. And when Lazarus is on the point of stepping out of the tomb, Jesus says (11: 40), 'Did I not tell you that, if only you had faith, you would see the glory of God?'

For St. John, therefore, the power and presence of God, the glory which is the essence of his being, are fully realized in the person and actions of the Word made flesh. But the supreme and final manifestation of this glory is to be seen, as the Evangelist interprets the course of events, in his crucifixion and death. Thus, as the hour of his passion approaches, Jesus announces to his disciples (12: 23), 'The hour has come for the Son of man to be glorified.' So far from attempting to conceal his meaning, he at once reminds them that a grain of wheat can only bear fruit if it has first been buried and allowed to rot in the earth, and that similarly the man who desires life must be prepared to surrender life. Later in the narrative, when Jesus is sitting with his disciples at the Last Supper, deeply troubled in spirit, and has warned them that one of them is going to betray him, we read that Judas departed to accomplish his design and that the Lord declared (13: 31), 'Now is the Son of man glorified, and in him God is glorified.' Here we have clearly expressed what has often been called the paradox of the Fourth Gospel, that Christ's willing abandonment of himself to humiliation and a shameful death is understood and delineated as his glorification, as the most compelling and significant disclosure of the divine glory which he shares with God the Father.

It is in keeping with this that St. John speaks of Christ's crucifixion as his exaltation or 'lifting up.' Early in his ministry the Lord had informed Nicodemus (3: 14) that, 'just as Moses lifted up the serpent in the wilderness, so must the Son of man be lifted up'; and in this sentence the verb employed deliberately carries the double meaning of being raised in glory and of being nailed to the upraised cross. Equally significant is the grim remark which he makes (8: 28) in argument with his critics, when they want to know who he really is: 'When you have lifted up the Son of man, then you will know that I am he.' Once again the crucifixion which he foresees will be his fate will also be the convincing demonstration of his oneness with the glory of the Father. Finally, we have his confident assurance (12: 32), 'I, when I am lifted up from the earth, shall draw all men to myself.' The casual reader might take this to mean that, when Christ has risen and ascended to heaven, he will exercise a universal attraction; but to guard against this the Evangelist inserts the cautionary note (12:33), 'He said this in order to indicate by what death he was going to die.' In other words, the revelation of divine glory which will bend the hearts and wills of men will not be Christ's triumphant ascent to the heavenly sphere (that of course will be its sequel), but his execution on the cross.

Although St. John does not spell the message out, it is evident that this interpretation of the passion involves a precious insight into the nature of God. In so far as the glory of God finds historical manifestation in the person of Jesus, and in so far as that glory is most completely expressed in his voluntary acceptance of humiliation, suffering and death, the Fourth Gospel presents a picture of God without parallel in any of the philosophies or theologies that men have contrived or wishfully speculated about. Voluntary suffering for others, self-surrender to death that others may live—these are modes of acting which belong, it would seem, to the eternal order. In the preceding chapter we observed that the New Testament, reversing our ordinary judgments, interprets the passion as springing from, and thus testifying to, the love of God; and while there is a tremendous affirmation implicit in this, it is one which at least falls within the range of our human understanding. Intrinsic to all true love is the element of sacrifice and self-giving. But the equation of shameful death with glory, and of suffering and humiliation with the radiant essence of God's being, issues in a far more startling paradox. For the man or woman who reads St. John's Gospel, and can enter into his inspired insight, not only must the passion, as an event in history, be transfigured, but an altogether new vista of life and of the values that are truly worth-while must open up.

8

THE NEW COMMUNITY

(i)

SO far we have considered several ways in which the New Testament writers understood the passion of Christ viewed in itself, in its inner motivation, and in its impact on the human situation. But they were no less convinced of the direct practical relevance of the events of Good Friday and Easter to believers; both they themselves and the Church were deeply and personally involved in them. The Messiah who suffered did not stand alone, isolated in Gethsemane and on the cross; nor was his resurrection the vindication and triumph of an individual martyr. Through his dying and rising again a new community had been brought into existence, pervaded and sustained by his Spirit. It was the new Israel, but it was also, in a real and profound sense, the body of Christ. And as it was his body, it seemed natural and indeed inevitable to the New Testament writers that it should bear the marks of his passion, just as that it should participate in the glory of his resurrection.

Thus the Christian community, the Church as it soon came to be called, was brought into existence through the Lord's passion and resurrection. There have been Christians who have sincerely held that the Church which emerged in the apostolic age, and has continued down the centuries, represents the grouping together of loyal disciples for mutual edification and for presenting the challenge of the Master's message to the world; but this is scarcely the New Testament explanation of its origin and nature. A more complete and accurate statement of this would be that in their view the Church is the new people of God, a people whom Christ has constituted by a covenant ratified by his blood and in whose midst he perpetually abides.

Centuries before the crucifixion, at Mount Sinai, the children of Israel had been formed into God's chosen people, and the covenant had been sealed by the blood of the sacrifices which (as we read in the graphic account of Exodus 24: 8) Moses had duly offered. At the Last Supper, according to the narratives of St. Mark (14: 24), St. Matthew (26: 28) and St. Paul (1 Cor. 11: 25), Jesus deliberately identified the blood which he knew he was shortly going to shed on the cross as the means whereby a new covenant was being sealed; and this covenant, as Jeremiah with inspired insight had predicted (31: 31-4), would be one bringing with it forgiveness, restoration and perfect fellowship with God. Consistently with this record, it is the Risen Christ, fresh from his passion and death, who announces to the Eleven (Matt. 28: 16-20) that all power has been given to him in heaven and on earth, who bids them go out into the world and make men and women of all nations into his disciples by baptizing them into the threefold name, and whose gracious promise is, 'Lo, I am with you always, until the close of the age.'

This conception of the Church as a new community taking its rise from the Lord's passion and resurrection is not confined to the Synoptic Evangelists and St. Paul. The First Epistle of Peter, for example, eloquently portrays (2: 9-10) Christians as the people of God, the object of his special choice and favour; but equally it makes it plain (2: 4-7) that the foundation of the spiritual house into which they are built 'like living stones' is the Christ whom men have rejected and crucified but God has gloriously vindicated. Again, according to the author of the Epistle to the Hebrews, Christians are brothers one to another (3: 1, 12), sanctified into one brotherhood with Christ, the high priest who offered propitiation for the sins of the people (2: 11-18). He also makes the point (9: 15-28) that, if Moses was the mediator of the old covenant which had proved ineffectual, Christ by his passion and death has been the mediator of the new and perfect covenant. In the theology of St. John Jesus is king, but of a kingdom which is 'not of this world' (John 18: 36); and its members are born, 'not of blood, nor of the will of the flesh, nor of the will of man, but of God' (John 1: 13). More precisely, their birth is through water and the Spirit (John 3: 5); and, as we saw in the preceding chapter, it is through his being lifted up on the cross that Jesus draws all men to himself. It is expedient, Jesus points out in this Gospel (16: 7), that he should leave his disciples, that is, go away from them to suffer and die, because only so the Paraclete, the Holy Spirit which binds the Church into unity and leads it into all truth, will come to them.

(ii)

Not surprisingly, therefore, the two great sacraments, the one by which men and women enter the Christian community, and the other by which they sustain their life in it and offer praise and glory to God for their redemption, are both in their different ways closely associated in the New Testament with the Lord's passion and resurrection. This is already anticipated in the mysterious reply which Jesus gave to James and John when, with naïve presumption, they had requested permission to sit, the one at his right hand and the other at his left, when the time for his enthronement in glory should come. His answer (Mark 10: 38–9) was that they apparently did not realize what they were asking for: were they able to drink the cup which he was drinking or to be baptized with his baptism? The mention side by side of the cup and of baptism was not fortuitous; the readers for whom the Gospel was written down were bound to interpret it as a reference, unintelligible to its first hearers but clear as day to themselves, to the two great sacraments which marked them off as disciples of the Lord. Jesus was not of course suggesting that James and John, or the countless believers of future generations of whom they were the prototypes, would be expected to suffer exactly the same fate as he. The implication was plain, however, that fellowship with him in his glory must entail fellowship with him in suffering and death as well (not necessarily or normally death on the cross, but an experience of which death was the appropriate analogy), and that baptism and the eucharist were the means by which they would express, and by regular communion renew, their participation in his passion.

The author of the Fourth Gospel had a similar understanding of the two sacraments, as is evident from his report (John 19: 34) that, when one of the soldiers pierced the side of the dead Jesus with his spear, 'there came out blood and water.' As many of the early Fathers of the Church accurately noted, these were in his eyes symbols of the eucharist and baptism respectively. Both the sacraments took their rise, and derived their inner significance, from the death of the Saviour.

No one is more explicit in working out this view of baptism than St. Paul, the New Testament theologian *par excellence* of this sacrament. Baptism, he teaches, initiates men and women into the Christian community, for (1 Cor. 12: 13) 'by one Spirit we were all baptized into one body,' that is, the body which is Christ's Church; and in baptism those 'who have been baptized into Christ have put on Christ' (Gal. 3: 27). By this he means that the baptized Christian has, as it were, been so clothed with Christ, or (to vary the metaphor) so caught up in him, that he is henceforth a new man in Christ (Eph. 4: 24; Col. 3: 10), or (as he expresses it even more incisively) 'a new creation' (2 Cor. 5: 17). But the presupposition of this vigorous imagery is his conviction that existentially baptism involves a mystical dying and rising again with the crucified Lord. This is made clear in a famous passage (Rom. 6: 3–4): 'All of us who have been baptized into Christ Jesus were baptized into his death. We were therefore buried with him as a result of our being baptized into his death, so that just as Christ was raised from the dead by the glory of the Father, we also might walk in a new form of life.'

In other words, the Pauline teaching is that our faith in Christ is not just our acceptance of him as Lord, nor even simply our commitment of ourselves to him as his devoted followers and servants. It involves, as a consequence of that faith expressed in the action of being baptized, so intimate a union between ourselves and Christ that in a real sense the man we previously were is done to death and a new man, 'conformed to the image of God's Son' (Rom. 8: 29), is brought into existence. A transformation has been effected, at the depth of our being, which can only be adequately described as our dying and rising again in such a way that we are now, as St. Paul characteristically phrases it, 'in Christ'; and the Church, or body of Christ, is the whole company of people, in all ages, who by this mystical dying and rising again in baptism are 'in Christ.'

Although St. Paul explores it most exhaustively, there is no reason to suppose that this understanding of the baptism which every Christian undergoes as his participation in Christ's passion and resurrection was confined to the Apostle. There is a difficult passage in the First Epistle of Peter (4: 1), where the writer impresses on his correspondents that, since Christ has 'suffered in the flesh' (by which he means that he has died), they too should arm themselves with the same thought, viz. that the man who has suffered in the flesh has finished with sin. Despite the obscurity of his language, it is likely that he is assimilating the experiences of the Asian Christians whom he is seeking to encourage (they too have died, but in their case the death is that of baptism) with the death, resurrection and triumph of their Master.

Deeply significant also are the accounts of the Lord's baptism by John which the three first Evangelists include near the beginning of their Gospels. All three describe how, as Jesus stepped out of the Jordan, the heavens opened and the voice of God acclaimed him, 'Thou art my only [or unique] Son.' This mode of address sounds strikingly like an echo of Genesis 22: 2, 12, 16, all passages in which Isaac, whom Abraham had been commanded to sacrifice, is spoken of as his 'only son.' There is evidence that in late Jewish writings Isaac was conceived of as the one perfect sacrifice by which the sins of Israel might be forgiven, the new high priest whom God would raise up and upon whom he would set his seal with the dramatic opening of the heavens. It was natural that primitive Christians familiar with this pattern of speculation should apply the Isaac imagery to Christ, and as they read the story should overhear sacrificial overtones in the utterance of the divine voice. In its original setting the voice marked out Jesus as the Son who, like Isaac, was prepared to go willingly to death on behalf of his brethren. But the Evangelists had theological as well as biographical motives for inserting the incident so prominently in the preludes to their Gospels. For their first readers the narratives recounted not only an interesting episode in the career of Jesus, but an experience which they had all had in their own baptism and to which the Lord's provided the clue. They too, as they stood in the water, had seen the heavens opened and had known themselves to be accepted as adoptive sons of God; and they too had been made aware that the sonship to which they had been thus admitted was one in which sacrificial suffering was an essential ingredient.

(iii)

If it is by baptism that Christians are admitted to the new community, it is by sharing in the eucharistic feast that they maintain their fellowship with one another and offer praise and glory to God. It is evident, from accounts in the Gospels which cannot be contradicted, that during his earthly lifetime Jesus was in the habit of enjoying table fellowship not only with his disciples but also with publicans and sinners. By so doing he brought to them the gracious presence of God and with it the forgiveness of sins. But while the meal which the Lord instituted at the Last Supper and which the Church has continued to observe down the ages must be seen in the context of these gatherings, it is equally clear that he invested it with a distinctive character all its own. Not only was it instituted, as St. Paul goes out of his way to emphasize (1 Cor. 11: 23), 'on the night in which he was being betrayed,' but all our narratives indicate, with interesting if perplexing differences of phrasing, that Christ in some way equated the bread and the wine with his body and blood, that is, with the sacrifice he was about to offer in order to establish and seal the new covenant. Thus from the start the eucharist has been inescapably associated with the Lord's passion; and here it may suffice to suggest three ways in which this becomes real in the life and worship of the believer.

First, it is obvious that when Christians celebrate the eucharist, they recall and commemorate, in the most dramatic manner, the sacrifice of Christ on the cross. In his account of the Last Supper St. Paul reports (1 Cor. 11: 25) that Christ gave the explicit instruction, 'Do this . . . as my memorial.' The words are not present in the Synoptic narratives, and they have often been treated as an interpolation of the Apostle's. This is, however, a highly implausible proposal; his narrative is not his own composition, but seems to reproduce a liturgical tradition handed down in the Church which he has himself received and with which he would scarcely have ventured to tamper. This is borne out by the fact that when, in the next verse (1 Cor. 11: 26), he comes to interpret the rite, he explains that 'as often as you eat this bread and drink the cup, you proclaim the Lord's death until he comes.' As a matter of fact, Christians have never doubted that in one of its principal aspects the eucharist is a commemoration of the passion. The tendency has rather been, in certain circles in comparatively recent times, to concentrate wholly on this aspect, and to take the view that Christ died for us on Calvary once for all, that at some future date he will come again and believers will be united with him, but that in the meantime we have a poignant reminder of his sacrificial death in the eucharistic symbols of his body and blood.

(iv)

The onesidedness and inadequacy of this approach come out when we observe, secondly, the New Testament conviction that in the eucharist Christians enjoy a real fellowship with the Lord who was crucified, died and rose again. It has often been argued that the formula 'This is my body' simply means, 'This bread represents, or is suggestive of, my body'; it is no more than a picturesque analogy, comparable with Christ's statement (John 15: 5), 'I am the vine, you are the branches.' St. Paul at any rate, however, manifestly understood the words of Jesus in a very realistic, and not merely symbolic, sense. Thus he warns (1 Cor. 11: 27) people who participate thoughtlessly in the sacred meal that they will be committing an offence against the Lord's body and blood, and insists (1 Cor. 11: 28–9) that the Christian ought to examine himself carefully before communion so as to be sure of 'distinguishing the body.' He is even more explicit in the previous chapter (1 Cor. 10: 16), where he asks, as if expecting unhesitating agreement, 'The cup of blessing which we bless, is it not a sharing in the blood of Christ? The bread which we break, is it not a sharing in the body of Christ?' Some have contended that he is not here speaking of communion with Christ's actual body, but of a spiritual union with the Christian community, which he also calls 'the body of Christ'; but this does violence to the whole context, and also overlooks his teaching that, in so far as the Church is the body of Christ, it is so precisely because it participates in his physical, though now glorified, body.

The point of this discussion, however, is not to raise again the exorcized ghosts (for exorcized we must hope they are by now) of the rival 'Catholic' and 'Protestant' approaches to sacramental theology. Their vitality has in large measure been due to the passion for excessive definition to which both sides have too willingly succumbed. The unbiassed student of scripture is surely bound to grant that in St. Paul's view

Christians who participate in the eucharist are uniting them-selves, or rather are being united, with Christ in his passion. Nor does St. Paul stand alone in the New Testament in teach-ing this doctrine. In his sixth chapter the author of the Fourth Gospel describes the miracle of the multiplication of loaves (6: 1–14), and from his manner of telling the story there can be no doubt that he has the eucharist in mind. Later in the same chapter he proceeds to recount the great discourse in which Jesus speaks of himself as the Bread of Life. 'I am the living bread,' he states (6: 51), 'which has come down from heaven. If any one eats this bread, he will live for ever; and the bread which I shall give for the life of the world is my flesh.' Almost immediately he adds (6: 53–6), 'Truly I tell you, unless you eat the flesh of the Son of man and drink his blood, you have no life in you. . . . He who eats my flesh and drinks my blood abides in me, and I in him.' Again the eucharistic atmosphere of the discourse is unmistakable. The flesh and blood referred to point to the Lord's sacrificial death, and the author clearly understands him to be implying that in the eucharist believers are sustained and enriched in their living fellowship with him by union with his sacrifice.

(v)

In the third place, the eucharist, in the thought of the New Testament writers, is the great sign of the Lord's resurrection. This is made quite evident in St. Mark's Gospel, which records his statement after his words over the cup (14: 25), 'Truly, I tell you, I shall not drink again of the fruit of the vine until that day when I drink it new in the kingdom of God.' The saying reveals that at the Supper Jesus was look-ing forward, beyond the death he was shortly to suffer, to the perfect fellowship of the consummated kingdom. It is an anti-cipation of this fellowship, made possible by the miracle of his resurrection and their own union with him, that Christians, likewise looking forward to the full coming of the kingdom, hopefully enjoy whenever they celebrate the eucharistic feast. This too is the key to St. Paul's statement (1 Cor. 11:26) quoted above that, when Christians eat the Lord's body and drink his blood, they proclaim his death *until he comes*. What is in his mind is that Christ is not dead but risen; it is his glorious body that is passed round at the holy supper, the crucified body that has been raised and transfigured by God's power and in which he will one day return. The eucharist thus looks back to the cross, but to the cross irradiated by the light of the resurrection and of the hope of the Saviour's coming again in glory.

A similar perspective is presented to us in St. Luke's narrative of the encounter of the two disciples journeying to Emmaus with the mysterious stranger. In fact it was the Risen Lord whom they met, but distressed as they were and convinced of his death they inevitably failed to recognize him. But the climax of the story comes when they halted at the village for the evening and invited their companion to join them at their supper. We read (Luke 24:30–31) that when he was at table with them, their guest took the bread and, after giving thanks, broke it and gave it to them. At once 'their eyes were opened and they recognized him; and he vanished out of their sight.' As the events are recorded, the two disciples seem to be ignorant of the Last Supper and of the eucharist; for them this was an ordinary meal, though one with an amazing sequel. But St. Luke, writing for the Church many years later, clearly intended to suggest that the incident was essentially a eucharistic celebration. For him, as his vocabulary in both the Gospel and Acts confirms, this was what 'the breaking of the bread' denoted. So in relating this episode he was not simply telling an edifying and remarkable story, but imparting to his fellow-Christians a theological lesson. The Scriptures, he is suggesting, lead us to Christ; all of them testify that Jesus, who died and rose again, is truly the Messiah foretold by the prophets. By studying and reflecting on them we can, if God so wills, attain the faith that Christ is our risen Saviour, alive for ever-more and in our midst. But if we are to recognize him and have fellowship with him face to face, risen and glorified as he is, the means he has appointed is 'the breaking of the bread.'

9

THE PATTERN OF DISCIPLESHIP

(i)

IF the new Christian community has been brought into existence by the Lord's death and resurrection, it is these events
which also determine its distinctive pattern of life. The earliest
name applied to the Christian movement, we discover from
the Acts of the Apostles (9: 2; 19: 9, 23; 22: 4; 24: 14, 22),
seems to have been 'the Way'; and although the origin of this
description remains obscure (some conjecture that it started
as an uncomplimentary title, almost equivalent to 'sect,' in
Greek-speaking Jewish circles), it very fittingly hints at the
entirely new, indeed revolutionary, attitude and behaviour
which marked out the first believers, and should characterize
their successors in all ages. This can be summarized in the convictions that, as servants of Christ who have died and risen
again with him in baptism, Christians are called to follow the
way of sacrificial love themselves, that they must tread this
road to the end in spite of all the tribulation and misunderstanding it is bound to entail, and that suffering thus cheerfully borne in union with the Crucified can have redemptive
meaning. This is an aspect of the passion without treatment of
which any discussion of these themes would be abstract and
theoretical to the point of impoverishment.

We may begin with the tradition of our Lord's sayings
reliably preserved in the Gospels. When Jesus selected his first
disciples, the two pairs of brothers, Simon and Andrew and
James and John, his summons was the peremptory command
(Mark 1: 17), 'Follow me'; and we read that 'immediately they
left their nets and followed him.' On a hasty reading we might
infer that 'following' has here the quite literal meaning of
'going after' or 'walking behind.' But the remainder of Jesus'

sentence (observe his supplementary remark, 'and I shall make you fishers of men') indicates that he has much more in prospect for them than that. In requesting them to 'follow' him, he is inviting them to become his disciples. Moreover, while Jesus must have given his contemporaries the impression that he was a rabbi or teacher, being one of his disciples involved much more than being the disciple or pupil of an ordinary rabbi did. It included, at the very least, close association with himself, joining in preaching his message, and exercising his powers in his name: so much is clear from, for example, the account given in Mark 3: 14–15.

On the eve of his betrayal Jesus invested the relationship with a still intenser, more personal quality by designating his disciples (John 15: 15) 'no longer . . . servants, but . . . friends,' on the ground that he has freely communicated to them everything he has himself heard from his Father. He has deliberately chosen his disciples so that they 'should go and bear fruit,' this fruit being the kind of life they have come to know through their regular companionship with him. He takes it for granted that they are to share his conditions of life and his destiny, for (Matt. 10: 24–5) 'the disciple is not above his teacher, nor a servant above his master; it is enough for the disciple to be like his teacher, and the servant like his master.'

(ii)

What discipleship involves, what the disciple has to look forward to, is spelled out, without any mincing of words, in many passages of the Gospels. Those who respond to Christ's call are to be ready to leave everything, whether possessions (Mark 10: 21), their customary occupations (Mark 2: 14), all economic security (Luke 9: 58), even where necessary their dearest family ties (Mark 10: 28–9). Hatred and contempt, open hostility, maltreatment and death itself may be their lot (Matt. 10: 16–23), but they need not be disheartened: the Holy Spirit is there to assist them (Matt. 10: 19–20), and in addition 'it has pleased the Father to give you the kingdom' (Luke 12: 32).

Most challenging, however, in this whole complex of sayings is the warning they convey about the inevitability of the cross. 'If any man wishes to come after me,' Jesus said (Mark 8: 34), 'let him deny himself and take up his cross and follow me'; and again (Luke 14: 27), 'Whoever does not bear his own cross and come after me cannot be my disciple.' There must be a radical abandonment of one's assertive ego, a crucifixion of the self and every kind of self-preoccupation. Yet along with this stand the promises that (Matt. 10: 39) 'he who loses his life for my sake shall find it,' and that (John 12: 24–6) the disciple who identifies himself with Christ by 'hating his life in this world' has the assurance that 'where I am, there shall my servant be also.'

It might be supposed that these sayings, particularly the 'hard' ones, were addressed primarily, or even exclusively, not to Christians in general, but to Jesus' special collaborators in his mission, to his disciples in the strict sense of that term. But this distinction cannot be sustained. Many of them, of course, appear to have been originally spoken to his immediate circle, but others (including such important ones as Mark 8: 34 quoted above) to the crowd as a whole together with the intimate group; while the solemn exhortation about denying oneself and taking up one's cross daily is clearly intended, in the form in which it is presented in Luke 9: 23, to be of universal application (cf. 'And he said to all . . . ').

Further, while during Jesus' earthly ministry a sharp line could be drawn between his regular associates and the more transitory hearers of his preaching, it is evident that this demarcation disappeared after his resurrection. Once that event had taken place, the narrower connotation of disciplehood ceased to be meaningful, and in the picture of the primitive communities drawn in Acts (for example, in 9: 10, 19, 36) all the faithful are without discrimination described as disciples. Still less do the New Testament documents suggest that the apostolic Church differentiated in any way between the fundamental moral and spiritual demands laid upon its various categories of members. As the Pastoral Epistles show, special aptitudes and special care in certain obvious spheres of conduct were naturally required of church officials; but the whole conception of a double standard in basic Christian living was a later intrusion, and represented a falling away from the primitive ideal. All Christians alike, however diverse their particular vocations in the community might be, were expected to manifest the same spirit of self-effacing service and mutual charity, the same readiness to sacrifice themselves and bear the blows of circumstance cheerfully, since all alike were servants of the invisible but ever-present Lord who guides the Church until the end of the world.

(iii)

The implications of this common pattern are nowhere sketched more simply and vividly than in the First Epistle of Peter. This letter is addressed, as we noted earlier, to a number of widely scattered congregations in Asia Minor (mainland Turkey, as it is to-day) which are having to face a great deal of misunderstanding and vilification, as well as positive ill-treatment, at the hands of their pagan neighbours, and its tone is pre-eminently pastoral. One of its leading themes is that Christians should accept suffering joyfully, for this is their proud vocation as followers of Christ. These congregations apparently include a high proportion of slaves, and these, just because they are Christians, find themselves victimized and bullied by their masters. The line the writer takes with them is instructive and worth reproducing. 'What credit is it,' he asks them (2: 20–21), 'if when you do wrong and are beaten for it you take it patiently? But if you take it patiently when you do right and suffer for it, then you have God's approval. For it is to this that you have been called, because Christ also suffered for you, leaving you an example, that you should follow in his steps.'

After this, drawing on the image of the Suffering Servant so poignantly depicted in Isaiah 53, he holds up before them the example of Christ, who trusting in God endured reviling and a shameful death without the least gesture of resentment, thereby securing our redemption. The slaves' painful experiences, he is suggesting, provide them with a magnificent opportunity for likewise triumphing over evil treatment and evil men by gentle acquiescence. This teaching becomes even clearer later in the letter, when he is envisaging in more general terms the animosity and possible violence to which his readers are exposed. Here his message is (4: 13ff.) that they should actually exult in their 'fiery ordeal' because it means that they are sharing in Christ's sufferings. They should in fact count themselves blessed to be reproached for Christ's name because God's Spirit rests upon them and they already participate (see 5: 1) in 'the glory that is to be revealed.'

This idea that Christians should take their suffering Master as their exemplar recurs repeatedly in the New Testament. St. Paul, for example, exhorts (1 Cor. 11: 1) his readers to 'be imitators of me, as I am of Christ,' and congratulates them (1 Thess. 1: 6) because they rejoiced in the Holy Spirit as a result of the afflictions in which their ready reception of the gospel landed them, and thus showed themselves 'imitators of myself and of the Lord.' So when he encourages the Roman Christians (Rom. 15: 1–3) to be tolerant of the failings of weaker brethren and not to be always out to please themselves, he points them to Christ as their model, who 'did not please himself, but, as it is written, "The reproaches of those who reproached thee fell on me".'

Similarly, when the author of the Epistle to the Hebrews seeks to revive his correspondents' drooping spirits and instil fresh faith and perseverance in them, he bids them (12: 2) 'look to Jesus, the pioneer and perfecter of our faith, who for the joy that was set before him endured the cross.' From the

First Epistle of John, too, we learn (2: 6) that any one who claims to 'abide in Jesus ought to walk in the same way as he walked,' and (3: 16) that the criterion of such imitation is our readiness to lay down our lives for our brothers as he has laid down his life for us. St. Paul, however, brings out with particular clarity that the imitation of Christ inculcated in the New Testament is not a matter of merely exterior similarity or conformity; the Christian, he writes (Phil. 2: 5ff.), should encourage the growth in himself of the identical 'mind,' or interior attitude, that Christ had when he humbled himself and 'became obedient to death, even death on a cross.'

As has already been explained in our treatment of baptism (pp. 77f.), the Pauline theology is very emphatic on this point: the life of Christians is regarded as a 'putting on' of Christ (Gal. 3: 27), a real participation in his death and resurrection as a result of which one's 'old man' is discarded and a 'new man' modelled on Christ is brought into existence (Eph. 4: 22–4; Col. 3: 9–10). So the Apostle can write (Rom. 14: 7–8), 'None of us lives to himself or dies to himself. If we live, we live to the Lord, and if we die we die to the Lord: so then, whether we live or die, we are the Lord's.' He himself, he is confident (Gal. 2: 19–20), is no longer alive as he was prior to his conversion: 'I have been crucified with Christ; and as a result it is no longer I who live, but Christ who lives in me.' Thus the life he now lives he lives 'by faith in the Son of God, who loved me and gave himself for me.' In his opinion (Rom. 8: 12–17) the man who is led by the Spirit of God, and has thus become God's son by adoption, should reckon suffering a privilege, for 'we suffer with him in order that we may be glorified with him.' Consistently with this, he can boast (Gal. 6: 17), probably with reference to the physical bruises he has received in the course of his tempestuous ministry, that he bears in his body 'the marks of Jesus.' Indeed the brutality and harsh treatment to which he is continually subjected cannot break his spirit because he knows (2 Cor. 4: 8–11) that, by enduring them in union with Christ, he is in effect reproducing in his own person the death of Jesus, and can be buoyed up with the assurance that the full and glorified life of Jesus will also be manifested in it.

(iv)

The passages cited above, selected as they are from many contexts and reflecting a great variety of situations, give us only momentary and partial glimpses into the mentality and attitude of Christians in the apostolic age. But there can be no question in our minds, when we study and ponder them, that their authors had grasped that the passion and resurrection were meant to be just as integral a part of their own experience as of Christ's. They were fully persuaded, as we have seen in earlier chapters, that the cross, in God's mysterious ordering of things, had immense and transforming significance for the whole human predicament. Equally, however, it was not something detached from or standing outside themselves, still less was it a mere symbol to be reverently contemplated and gratefully accepted because of the amazing work which Christ had accomplished through it. On the contrary, they seem to have taken it for granted that that work must remain only half completed, and could not reach its final goal, until Christ's disciples had themselves embraced the cross, had taken it into their personal lives, and had made it the mainspring of all their thinking, willing and acting. Then, and only then, could the new and glorious life which God has offered to the world in the passion of his Son become a blessed reality.

This in essence is the practical message, painful but wonderfully transfiguring, which the New Testament delineation of the passion proclaims to men and women in every age. The world of the forties to the eighties of the first century, when most of the New Testament books were composed, was in countless respects different from the world we know in the seventies of the twentieth century. If we could, by some miracle, be transported back in time, the superficial aspect of daily life would surprise and bewilder us. A whole multitude of things, from habits of behaviour to modes of thinking, from social, political and economic arrangements to instinctive beliefs and presuppositions, would seem strange and unrecognizable. Yet as we became habituated to the altered atmosphere, we should discover that almost all these initially astounding discrepancies concerned only the surface of these two widely separated epochs. Fundamentally, in those areas of human existence which really matter, particularly in the obstinate problems with which every human being has to wrestle, we should find the similarities much more impressive. The struggle between good and evil, for justice and decency in human relations and for the dignity of the human person, is just as embittered, protracted and frustrating now as then. Fortuitous disasters affecting whole communities, unmerited suffering striking blameless individuals, tragic bereavements, outbursts of malevolent and senseless violence—all these are just as frequent in their incidence as then. Famine and disease, the exploitation of man by man and havoc-spreading wars remain the scourges they have always been; and in spite of the spectacular achievements of science, technology and medicine, unhappiness abounds, and the spectre of death stands awaiting each one of us.

These obdurate facts present enigmas which no merely rational philosophy has been able to solve, still less render palatable. Even thinkers who believe in the providence of God have to confess themselves baffled, for the difficulty of squaring the goodness of an omnipotent Creator with the misery and apparent irrationality of the world continues to elude them. We begin to see light, however, when as Christians we come to accept the gospel teaching that behind the cross stands the love of God—God reconciling the world to himself, and overcoming the evil in it, by the passion of his Son. And that glimmering light breaks into a blaze of glory when, taking the Master at his word, we put our own shoulders to his cross, let our hands and feet be nailed to it, and allow its influence to invade, penetrate and dominate our being.

The power which flows into us from it certainly does not eliminate the harsh realities which perplex and hurt us. Pain cuts as sharply and deeply for the Christian as for others, disappointment is as real and bitter, the spite and callousness of his fellow-men are no less humiliating and destructive. As Jesus remarked to his disciples (John 14: 27), he gives us peace, but not peace as the world understands it. But through our fellowship with the Crucified, through our abandonment of ourselves to him and our voluntary participation in his cross, we have already entered on a new dimension of existence. We have not escaped from the world and its cruelties, still less have we found refuge in a dream-house of wishful fantasy; but two amazing things have happened. First, the cross and the love of God it radiates enable us to view the entire aspect of things in a new perspective; and, secondly, when we confront the evil in men with the sacrificial compassion of the cross, we find it has power to exert, bit by bit, its transforming effect. We begin to understand what the Lord meant when he said (John 16: 33), 'In the world you have tribulation; but be of good cheer, I have overcome the world.'